D1508860

NESARA I

National Economic Security

and Reformation Act

Maine-Patriot.com
3 Linnell Circle
Brunswick, Maine 04011

maine-patriot.com

NESARA I

NESARA I

National Economic Security and Reformation Act

Contents

Background

NESARA I

"SIC FULGET IN UMBRAS"
"TRUTH IS ENVELOPED IN OBSCURITY"

NESARA I

Background
About NESARA

Throughout history many prophets have come forth... but change is on the horizon. The power grab of the elite is coming to an end.

With all their power and money, the bankers thought themselves to be above the law. But cracks were now appearing in their foundations. Angry Americans were beginning to fight back.

A Class Action Lawsuit was brewing, which would thereafter change the balance of power. This change began in the mid 1970's when the Federal Land Bank illegally foreclosed on farmers' mortgages all throughout the Midwest. In each of these cases, the farmers were defrauded by the banks, with the approval of the Federal Reserve System. These court cases would become known as the Farmer Claims Program.

In 1978 an elderly ranch farmer in Colorado purchase a farm with a loan from the Federal Land Bank. After he died, the property was passed on to his son, Roy Schwasinger, Jr. who was a retired military General. Soon after a Federal Land Bank officer and a federal Marshal appeared on his property and informed him that the bank was foreclosing on his farm, and to vacate it within 30 days.

Without his knowledge his deceased father had signed a stipulation which reverted the property back to the Federal Land Bank in the event of the borrower's death.

Outraged, Roy Schwasinger filed a class-action lawsuit in the Denver Federal Court system. But the case didn't go very far, and the suit was dismissed for filing incorrectly. This began Roy Schwasinger's investigation into the inner workings of the banking system.

In 1982, he was given a contract by the US Senate and later the Supreme Court, to investigate banking fraud. But because he was under a strict non-disclosure order, he was not allowed to tell anyone what he had discovered.

In the late 80's he began sharing his knowledge with others, including high-ranking military personnel, who helped bring about a class-action lawsuit against the Federal Government. (CV920C-1781 93Jun.2)

The 1st series of those loses began in the 1980's when William and Shirley Baskerville, of Fort Collins, Colorado were involved in a bankruptcy case with First Interstate Bank of Fort Collins, that was trying to foreclose on their farm.

At a restaurant, their lawyer informed them that he would no longer be able to help them, and walked off. Overhearing the conversation, Roy Schwasinger offered his advice on how to appeal the case in Bankruptcy Court.

So in 1987, they filed an appeal with the United States District Court in Colorado.

On December 3rd, 1988, the Denver Federal Court System ruled that, indeed, the banks had defrauded the Baskervilles and proceeded to reverse its bankruptcy decision, but when the foreclosed property was not returned, they filed a new lawsuit. Eventually 23 other Farmers, Ranches, and Indians, swindled by the bank, in the same manner, would join in the case.

(US District Court For The District Of Colorado, CV-92-C-1781).

In these cases the banks were foreclosing on the properties using fraudulent methods such as charging exorbitant interest, illegal foreclosure, or by not crediting mortgage payments to their account, as they should have, but instead, would steal the mortgage payments for themselves, triggering foreclosure on the properties.

After running out of money they continued their fight without the help of lawyers. With some assistance by the Farmers Union a new lawsuit was filed against the Federal Lane Bank and the Farm Credit System.

The District Court ruled in their favor and ordered the banks to return the stolen properties with help from either Federal Marshals or the National Guard, but when no payments were made, the farmers declared involuntary chapter 7 bankruptcy against the Federal Land Bank and Farm Credit System.

The banks appealed their case, insisting that they were not a business but a federal agency, therefore they were not liable to pay the damages, so the farmers legal team adopted a new strategy.

According to the Federal Land Bank 1933 Charter, they are not allowed to make loans directly to applicants, but instead, could only back loans as a guarantee in case of default.

Because the Federal Land Bank had violated this rule, the farmers' legal team was able to successfully sue the bank for damages.

Word of the lawsuit began to spread. The legal team would teach others how to fight foreclosure and help them file lawsuits as well, so celebrities such as Willy Nelson joined in the case and helped raise money during his Farm Aid concerts.

Here is a short clip of Willy Nelson describing in his own words the series of events leading up to the Farmer Claims legal case.

"This whole thing started when agriculture collapsed. The housing thing came second. Gee, I've been in Farm Aid a long time, and I've been seeing farmers leave the farm. There was 8 million family farms, and now there are less than 2 million, losing 300-500 a week."

"The reason they're going is because they're going out and taking the land back, and now they're taking the houses back that they stole."

"I mean, they told the farmers to plant fence post to fence post . . . We'll take care of you, buddy . . . and loaned him more money than he could pay back, and then he winds up loosing his farm."

"Same thing happened to the house owners. Loaned him more money that he can pay back, then the next thing you know, and the government's got all the land, and all the money, and we just gave the assholes 6 or 7 more billion dollars!"

The Baskerville case had now become the Farmer Claims class action lawsuit.

Worried about the legal ramifications, the government retaliated against the farmers by hitting them with either outrageous IRS fees or by imprisoning the legal team under frivolous non-related charges. When the farmers realized they were being unfairly targeted, they and military generals, such as General Roy Schwasinger, sat in the court room to make sure that the bribed judges would vote according to constitutional law.

The farmers now with a large versus in knowledgable people filed a case to claim additional damages from the fraudulent loan activities of the Farmer Credit System.

The government tried to settle, but they had lost many cases and were now losing their appeals as well. More and more evidence was collected.

According to the National Banking Act all banks were required to register their charter with the Federal and State Bureau of Records, but none of the banks had complied, allowing the legal team to sue the Farmer Credit System.

No only was the Farmer Credit System not chartered to do business with the Banking Association, but similar American quasi government organizations such the FHA, HUD, and even the Federal Reserve Bank.

The Farmer Claims lawsuit was thrown out of court at each level, with the Records purposely destroyed, so in the early 1990's, Roy Schwasinger brought the case before the United States Supreme Court. Some of the content of this was sealed from the public eyes, but most of it can be readily seen today.

Almost unanimously the US Supreme Court Justices ruled that the Farmers Union Claims were indeed valid.

Therefore all property foreclosed by the Farmer Claims System was illegal, and those who were foreclosed on would have to receive damages.

In all, they ruled that the Federal Government and banks had defrauded the farmers *and all United States Citizens* out of vast sums of money and property.

Furthermore, the Court ruled the shocking truth that the IRS was a Puerto Rican trust, that the Federal Reserve was unlawful, that the income tax amendment was only ratified by 4 states, and therefore was not a legal amendment, and that the IRS Code was not enacted into positive law within the code of Federal Regulations, and how the federal government illegally forerclosed on farmers homes with the help from federal agencies.

Irrefutable proof was presented by a retired CIA agent. He provided testimony and records of the bank's illegal activities to leave further evidence that the Farmer Union's claims were in fact legitimate. The implications of such a decision were profound. All gold, silver and property titles taken by the Federal Reserve and the IRS must be returned to the people.

The legal team sought assistance from a small group of benevolent visionaries consisting of politicians, military generals, and business people, who had been secretly working to restore the Constitution since the 1950's. Somehow, within their ranks, a four-star Army

General received high honors receiving the original 1933 US Bankruptcy proceedings. And when the case was brought before the US Supreme Court they ruled in his favor giving the Army General title over the United States, Inc.

Legal action was *then* passed on to the Senate Finance Committee and Senator Sam Nunn who was working with Roy Schwasinger.

"I will tell you the price of buying back the United States Government: it's $500 million dollars a year. In the early 90's Newt Gingrich and the republicans got together their plan, its now on the streets, its been exposed by a Columbia professor; they concluded that they could buy the United States Government for $300 million dollars a year, and by golly they did" — S. Nunn.

With the help from covert congressional and political pressure, President George Herbert Walker Bush issued an Executive Order on October 23, 1991, *Principles of Ethical Conduct for Government Officers and Employees,* which provided a provision allowing anyone who had a claim against the Federal Government to receive a payment as long as it's within the rules of the original fundamentals of the case.

According to the Federal Reserve Act of 1913, "All present and succeeding debt against the US Treasury must be assumed by the Federal Reserve." Thus the farmers' legal team was able to use that Executive Order to not only force the Federal Reserve to pay our damages in a gold backed currency but to allow them to receive legal ownership over the bankruptcy of the United States, Inc.

To collect damages, the farmers' legal team used an obscure attachment to the 14th Amendment, which most people are not aware of.

After the Civil War, the Government allowed citizens to claim a payment on anyone who suffered damages as a result of the Federal Government for failing to protect its citizens from harm of damages by a foreign government.

President Ulysses S. Grant had this attachment sealed from public eyes, but somehow someone on the farmers' legal team, got a hold of it. If you listen to that carefully, it specifies damages by a foreign government. That foreign government is the corporate Federal Government which has been masquerading to the public as the Constitutional Government.

Remember, this goes back to the organic Act of 1871 and the Trading with the Enemy Act of 1933 which defined all citizens as enemy combatants under the federal system known as THE UNITED STATES.

The Justices and farmers' legal team recognized how evil and corrupt our federal government had become and to counteract this they added some provisions in the settlement to bring the Federal Government under control.

First, they would have to be paid using a lawful currency backed by gold and silver as the Constitution dictates. This would eliminate their influence and gyrating economic cycles created by the Federal Reserve System.

Second, they would be required to go back to Common law instead of Admiralty law under the gold fringed flags. Under Common law if there is no damage done, or harm done, then there is no violation of the law. This would eliminate millions of laws which are used to control the masses and protect corrupt politicians.

Lastly, the IRS would be dismantled and replaced with a national sales tax

This is the basis of the NESARA law.

When the legal team finally settled on a figure, each individual would receive an average of $20 million dollars payout per claim. Multiplied by a total of 336,000 claims that are filed against the US Federal Government, the total payout will come out to a staggering $6.6 trillion dollars.

The US Supreme Court placed a gag-order on the case and struck all information from the Federal Registry and placed all of the records in the Supreme Court Files, up to that point.

Senator Sam Nunn kept the Baskerville Court Case within his office.

A settlement was agreed to out of court and the decision was sealed by Attorney General Janet Reno.

Because the case was sealed, claimants were not allowed to share Supreme Court Case documents with the media without violating the settlement, but they could still tell others about the lawsuit. This is probably why you haven't heard about this.

In 1991 General Roy Schwasinger went before a Senate Committee to present evidence of the bank's and the government's criminal activity. He informed them of how the corporation of the United States was tied to the establishment of the New World Order which would bring about a Fascist One Word Government ruled by the international bankers.

So in 1992, a task force was put together consisting of over 300 retired, and 35 active US Military Officers who strongly supported constitutional law.

Among them where, Admiral Jeremy M. Boorda, Chief of Naval Operations; William E. Colby, Director of the CIA, and General David J. McCloud, United States Air Force.

This Task Force was responsible for investigating government officials, Congressional officers, Judges, and the Federal Reserve.

They uncovered the common practice of bribery and extortion committed by both senators and judges.

"And every single member of Congress is impeachable for having abdicated their Article I responsibilities under the Constitution and serving as foot soldiers for the President and his mendacious Vice President."

The criminal activity was so rampant that only two out of 535 men were deemed honest, but more importantly they carried out the first ever audit of the Federal Reserve.

The Federal Reserve was used to giving out orders to politicians and had no intentions of being audited, however, after they were informed that their offices would be raided, under military gunpoint if necessary, they complied with the investigation.

After reviewing their files, the military officers found

$800 trillion dollars sitting in their accounts which should have been applied to the National Debt, and contrary to federal government propaganda, they also discovered that in fact most nations owed money to the United States, instead of the other way around.

These hidden trillions were then confiscated and placed into European bank accounts in order to generate the enormous funds needed to pay the Farmer Claims class action lawsuit. Later, this money would become the basis of the Prosperity Programs.

Despite these death blows, President George H. W. Bush and the illuminati continued on with their plan of Global Enslavement.

"When we are successful, and we will be, we have a real chance at this New World Order, an Order in which a credible United Nations can use its peace keeping role to fulfill the promise and vision of the United Nations Founders." — George Bush, Sr.

In August of 1992, the military officers confronted President Bush, and demanded that he sign an agreement that he would return the United States to Constitutional Law, and ordered him to never use the term New World Order again.

Bush pretended to cooperate, but secretly planned to bring about the New World Order, anyway, by signing an Executive Order, on Dec. 25, 1992, that would have in effect closed all banks, giving Bush an excuse to declare martial law. Under the chaos of martial law, Bush intended to install a new Constitution which would have kept everyone currently in office in their same position for 25 years, and it would have removed all rights to elect new officials.

The military intervened and stopped Bush from signing that military order.

In 1993, members of the Supreme Court, certain members of Congress, and representatives from the Clinton government met with high ranking US military officers who were demanding a return to Constitutional law, reforms of the banking system and financial redress. They agreed to create the Farmer Claims Process which would allow the legal team to set up meetings all over the country on a grassroots level, to help others file claims and to educate them about the law suit.

A claim of harm can be made on any loan issued by any financial institution, for all interest paid, foreclosures, attorney and court fees, IRS taxes or liens, Real Estate and property taxes, mental and emotional stress caused by the loss of property, stress related illnesses such as suicide and divorce, and even warrants, incarceration, and probation, could also be claimed.

But the Clinton government undermined their efforts by requiring the farmer claimants to use a specific form designed by the government. This form imposed an administration fee of $300 for each claim, which was later used in 1994 as a basis to arrest the leaders of the legal team, including Roy Schwasinger. The government was so afraid of what they would say during their trial in Michigan, that extra steps were taken to conceal the true nature of the case.

County Courthouse employees were not allowed to work between Monday and Thursday during the course of the trial, and outside the Court House, FBI agents formed a perimeter preventing the media and visitors from learning what was going on, as well.

Harassment and retaliation by the government increased. Many were sent to prison, or murdered while incarcerated. Despite being protected by his military personnel, the Army General who had acquired the original 1933 title of Bankruptcy of the United States was imprisoned, killed, and replaced with a clone. This clone was then used as a decoy to prevent any further claims from being filed.

During the 1st Clinton administration, the military delayed many of Clinton's federal appointments until they were sure that these federal individuals would help restore Constitutional law. One such individual who promised to bring about the necessary changes was attorney General Janet Reno.

"If Bill and Hillary Clinton come and tell Web Hubble to tell me to do something wrong, I'm going to say, well tell him I'm not going to do it."

In agreement with the Supreme Court ruling, on June 3rd, 1993, Janet Reno ordered the Delta Force and Navy Seals to Switzerland, England, and Israel to recapture trillions of dollars of gold stolen by the Federal Reserve System from the strategic gold reserves.

These nations cooperated with the raid because they were promised their debts owed to the United States would be cancelled, and because the people who stole money from the United States also stole money from their nations as well. This bullion is to be used for the new currency backed by precious metals.

It is now safely stockpiled at the NORAD [North American Aerospace Defense command] complex in Colorado Springs, Colorado, and four other repositories.

Janet Reno's actions so enraged the powers-that-be, that it resulted in her death. She was then replaced with a clone, and with this creature who was responsible for covering up the various claim scandals. To keep the Secretary of the Treasury, Robert Rubin, in line, he too was also cloned. For their remainder in public office, both Reno and Rubin received their salaries from the International Monetary Fund [IMF], as foreign agents, and not from the US Treasury.

Despite these actions the legal team continued on with their fight while managing to avoid bloodshed and a major revolution.

After 1993, the Farmer Claims process name was changed to Bank Claims. Between 1991 and 1996 the US Supreme Court required US Citizens to file bank claims to collect damages, paid by the US Treasury Draft, This process closed in 1996.

During this time, the US Supreme Court signed one or more Justices to monitor the progress of the rulings. They enlisted the help of experts in economics, monetary systems, banking, constitutional government and law, and then in other related areas. These Justices build coalitions of support and assistance with thousands of people worldwide, know as White Knights.

The term White Knights was borrowed from the world of big business. It refers to a vulnerable company that is rescued by a corporation or a wealthy person from a hostile takeover.

To implement the required changes, the five Justices spent years negotiating how the reformations would occur. Eventually they settled on certain agreements, also known as "Accords", with the US Government, the Federal Reserve [Bank] owners, the IMF, the World Bank, and with numerous other countries, including the United Kingdom, and countries of the Euro Zone.

Because these banking reformations will impact the entire world, the IMF, World Bank, and other countries had to be involved. The reformations required that the Federal Reserve be absorbed by the US Treasury Department and the Banks' fraudulent activities must be stopped, and payment must be paid for past harm.

In 1998, the military Generals who were originally participated in the Farmer Claims process realized that the US Supreme Court Justices had no intentions of implementing the Accords, so they decided that the only way to implement the reformation was through a law passed by Congress.

In 1999, a 75 page document known as the National Economic Security and Reformations Act (NESARA) was submitted to Congress where it sat with little action for almost a year.

Late one evening, on March 9, 2000, a written quorum call was hand delivered by Delta Force and Navy Seals to 5 members of the US Senate and the US House who were sponsors and cosponsors of NESARA. They were immediately escorted by the Delta Force and Navy Seals to their respective voting chambers where they passed the National Economic Security and Reformation Act. [NESARA]

These five members of Congress were the only people who were lawfully allowed to hold office in accordance with the original 13th Amendment.

Remember, British soldiers destroyed copies of the Titles of Nobility Amendment in the War of 1812 because it prevented any one who had ties to the Crown of England from holding public office.

NESARA is the most ground-breaking Reformation to sweep, not only this country, but our planet, in its entire history. The Act does away with the Federal Reserve Bank, the IRS, the shadow government, and much, much more.

NESARA implements the following changes:

1. Zeroes out all credit card, mortgage, and other bank debt due to illegal banking and investment activities. This is the Federal Reserve's worst nightmare, a Jubilee for Forgiveness of debt.

2. Abolishes the income tax.

3. Abolishes the IRS. Employees of the IRS will be transferred into the US Treasury National Sales Tax area.

4. Creates a 14% flat rate on non-essential "new items only" sales tax revenue for the government. In other words, food and medicine will not be taxed. Nor will used items, such as old homes.

5. Increases benefits for senior citizens.

6. Returns Constitutional Law to all courts and legal matters.

7. Reinstates the original Title of Nobility Amendment. Hundreds of thousand Americans under the control of foreign powers will lose their citizenship, be deported to other countries, and barred from reentry for

the remainder of their life. And millions of people will discover that their college degrees are now worthless paper.

8. Establishes new Presidential and Congressional elections, within 120 days after NESARA's announcement. The interim government will cancel all national emergencies and return us back to constitutional law.

9. Monitors elections and prevents illegal election activities of special interest groups.

10. Creates a new US Treasury rainbow currency backed by gold, silver, and platinum precious metals. Ending the bankruptcy of the United States initiated by Franklin Delano Roosevelt in 1933.

11. Forbids the sale of American Birth Certificate Records as chattel property bonds, by the US Department of Transportation.

12. Initiates a new US Treasury Bank System in alignment with Constitutional Law.

13. Eliminates the Federal Reserve System. During the transition period, the Federal Reserve will be allowed to operate side by side of the US Treasury for one year, in order to remove all Federal Reserve Notes from the money supply.

14. Restores financial privacy.

15. Retrains all judges and attorneys in Constitutional Law.

16. Ceases all aggressive US Government military actions world wide.

17. Establishes peace throughout the world.

18. Releases enormous sums of money for humanitarian purposes.

19. Enables the release of over 6,000 patents of suppressed technologies that are being withheld from the public, under the guise of national security, including free energy devises, antigravity and sonic healing machines.

"I want the American people to know today that I am still committed to working with people of good faith and good will of both parties to do what's best for our country." — President William Clinton.

Because President Clinton's clone had no interest in signing NESARA into law, on October 10, 2000, under orders from the US Military Generals, the elite Naval Seals and Delta Force stormed the White House and then, at gunpoint, forced Bill Clinton to sign NESARA into law.

During this time the Secret Service and the White House security personnel were ordered to stand down and were disarmed, and allowed to witness this event under a gag order.

From its very inception, Bush, Sr., the Corporate government, major bank houses, and the Carlyle Group have opposed NESARA.

To maintain secrecy the case details and the docket number were sealed and revised within the official Congressional Registry to reflect a commemorative coin, and then, again, it was revised even more recently. This is why there are no public Congressional records, and why a search for this law will not yield the correct details, until after the Reformations are made public.

You probably never heard of this law due to an extremely strict gag order placed upon politicians, media personnel, and bank officers.

Even though Alex Jones or Ron Paul will not tell you about it, the law is still valid, and members of Congress will not tell us any of this, because they have been ordered by the Supreme Court Justices to deny the existence of NESARA or face charges of treason punishable by death.

Some members of Congress have been actually charged with obstruction of justice.

"We're here to the nation's capital to tell the story that we've got an economic convulsion in agriculture; we've got a lot of broken dreams, a lot of broken families, a lot of broken lives, and we're not going to take it an longer."

Minnesota Senator Paul Wellstone was about to break the gag order, but before he could, his small passenger plane crashed killing his wife, daughter, and himself. If this isn't enough to keep Congress in line, money is. The CIA routinely bribes Senators with stolen loot from the Bank Roll programs. Every Senator has been bribed with a minimum of $200 million dollars deposited into a Bank of America account in Canada.

You will never hear the media networks report about NESARA. To maintain silence, major news networks, such as CNN, are paid to the tune of $2 billions dollars annually.

Some of this loot is funneled by the Mormon Church in Utah through Senator Orrin Hatch's office and Bank of America.

Not only is Congress bribed, but the entire Joint

Chiefs of Staff, and the upper tier of the government, including the President himself, receive these payments as well. Only the Provost Marshal has the lawful authority to arrest these individuals, but sadly, he won't do his job either. It seems the United States Military is full of pencil pushing politicians who care more about advancement than doing their jobs, and not surprisingly, much dis-information about NESARA can be found on the Internet.

Prominent naysayers include *quartloos.com* which is rumored to be a CIA front; *nesara.org,* which is maintained by the Bush family; Sherry Shiner and various internet channelers, receiving their messages from psychopathic spooks, have all contributed to the confusion.

Even the information of Wikipedia is in error. Wikipedia gives you the history of CIA agent Harvey Barnard's NESARA law. If you look closely, this law stands for the **National Economic Stabilization and Recovery Act** which would have made reforms to the economy to replace the Income Tax with a national sales tax. This law was rejected by Congress in the 1990's. But there is little mention of the **National Economic Security and Reformation Act** on Wikipedia, or its ramifications.

The next step is to announce NESARA to the world, but its not an easy task to do. Many powerful groups have tried to prevent the implementation of NESARA.

The NESARA Law requires that at least once a year an effort be made to announce the law to the public. Three current US Supreme Court Judges control the committee in charge of NESARA's announcement. These judges have used their overall authority to seek to sabotage its announcement.

In 2001, after much negotiation, the Supreme Court Justices ordered the current Congress to pass resolutions approving NESARA. This took place on September 9, 2001, 18 months after NESARA become law. On September 10, 2001, George Bush Sr. moved into the White House to steer his son on how to block the announcement.

The next day, on September 11, 2001, at 10:00 AM, EDT, Allan Greenspan was scheduled to announce the new US Treasury Bank System, debt forgiveness for all US Citizens, and the abolishment of the IRS, as a first part of the public announcement of NESARA.

Just before the announcement, at 9:00 AM, Bush Sr. ordered the demolition of the World Trade Center, to stop the international banking computers on floors one and two, in the North Tower, from initiating a new US Treasury Bank System.

Explosives in the World Trade Center were planted by the CIA, and Mossad operatives, and detonated remotely in building 7, which was demolished later that day, in order to cover up their crime.

Remote pilot technology was used in a fly-over event to deliver a payload of explosives into the Pentagon, at the exact location of the White Knights, at their new Naval Command Center, who were coordinating activity supporting NESARA's implementation, nationwide.

With the announcement of NESARA stopped dead in its tracks, George Bush Sr. decapitated any hopes of returning the government back to the people.

While CIA agent, Osama Ben Laden, is made into the boogy man, the country dashed off to fight a war on terror.

The events of 911 eventually led the way to the slaughter of the Iraqi people. To keep the public unaware of the carnage, the official death count of US soldiers and Iraqi civilians is purposely under reported.

Deceased US soldiers are either being dumped into the Persian Gulf, or replaced with clones. As of 2009 the total death count of Iraqi civilians now surpasses a staggering 1.6 million people!

The same cooked statistics apply to the death totals on the day of 911. According to the government, 2,752 people died that day, when in actuality, 30,700 people had died.

No one questions the insanely small numbers given out by the government, because New York City is a large place. People with lost loved ones do not make contact with others, so they have no way of knowing actually how many people have died.

WAR ON TERROR CASUALTIES REPORT
[Not For Public Release]
DOD ID: 179BR82
Office of the Chairman
The Joint Chiefs of Staff
Washington, DC 20319-9999

The Bush family was originally offered $300 trillion dollars to cooperate with NESARA but instead they chose to maintain their control over us; so in the end, the Bush family will end up with nothing.

The Attacks of 911 had managed to stop the announcement of NESARA dead in its tracks. Many more attempts have been made over the years but the Bush family has managed to stop them.

These people won't be able to get away with their crimes forever. Little by little their wealth is being dismantled right before their eyes.

Before NESARA is announced to the public it was stipulated that the original Farmer Claims, first be paid out, with a bullion backed currency issued by the US Treasury. In other words, they cannot be paid in Federal Reserve Notes.

The $6.6 trillion dollar Farmer Claims payout is to be distributed in the form of ATM Debit Cards. Remember, this money will come from the Bank Rolls and Prosperity Programs. The only catch is that to distribute these funds they must first be released by the trustees whose members come from the Clinton, Bush, and Rockefeller families.

They are doing everything they possibly can to stop these payouts.

One way is to transport the banking documents, which contain instructions on how to access these funds, in a never ending loop, 24/7, between warehouses in Charlotte North Carolina, and Washington DC. The drivers of these Fed Ex Trucks are heavily bribed, and many of them are afraid of being arrested by the Department of Homeland Security if they were actually to deliver their payload, as required by law.

At one point, after the packages were returned to Washington DC, President George W. Bush placed them under military quard. Federal Judges ordered him to release the funds, but Bush [the younger], replied, *"You will never receive these packages, they belong to me."*

The judge answered, *"I can do no more; he is the President of the United States."* The only option left is to arrest the President, but the police commissioner, the Provost Marshal, and the military, refuse to help.

This cycle has been ongoing for years. The only alternative left is to kill the Federal Reserve System by force. The problem is that George Bush, and now Obama, have threatened to use the dollar as a weapon of mass destruction against the nations of the world, to comply with the New Word Order agenda.

Bush once commented, *"The people will now suffer greatly."*

The world cannot tolerate this. The dollar must be removed as the international world's currency, and replaced with a new independent assets based monetary unit backed by precious metals.

On December 15, 2006, a meeting was arranged to discuss ways to curtail these criminal activities. Their ranks included representatives from the global family who were enlightened individuals working directly under Saint Germain. They include members from the IMF, the World Bank, the Rothschild family, and key persons from over 48 nations.

They agreed to implement *three goals* by June 15, 2007, that is [1] to end all war, [2] to actively improve the environment, and [3] to actively provide abundance for their people.

Those nations which will not keep this agreement will eventually be cut off from the international banking community in order to force them into compliance.

On September 19, 2007, a new global banking system was approved by Congress.

On October 19, 2007, at midnight, the US Treasury of the Republic went on line with a new gold backed banking system, but this gold banking system is not being deployed, because the banks are trying to dispose of their worthless derivatives before they get set to zero, when the new gold backed currency valuations go into force.

To improve the stability of the banking system, in 1988 the BIS implemented Basel I, which required banks to hold 6% net capital. On December 1st, 2007, this went a step further, when Basel II was implemented, requiring all loans to be backed by the appropriate collateral, and raise net capital requirements to 8%.

The new rules prevent the bankers from collateralizing their derivatives with stolen money from collateral accounts and Prosperity funds. Furthermore, all assets must be valued according to the daily market price, also know as the "market to market" rule.

Any bank which refuses to comply with Basel II will be cut off from international markets, which is why American banks demanded $700 billion dollars from the *Troubled Asset Relief Program.* If they didn't get this bailout, the banks would have shut their doors, inciting Marshal Law.

On June 15, 2009, Basel III was initiated which goes a step further than Basel II, by requiring the banks to disclose any previously undisclosed junk assets, or derivatives marked off the balance sheet.

Jack Blog has investigated financial fraud for the federal government, for over 30 years. He has found that the banks use off balance sheet financial operations to hide money in places like the Caymen Islands.

"If a bank, for example, has done bad lending, they put it in a portfolio of an offshore entity. No one will be able to figure out what that offshore entity is worth, and its that kind of transaction that has actually disabled the world financial system. I think every bank at this point should be forced to come absolutely clean about how much money it has in these offshore shells, of different kinds, and how many deals more are hidden in the balance sheets and on the books."

Under Basel III, every bank transaction must be disclosed on the balance sheet. But if this were to happen, these banks would become insolvent over night, and would not be able to pass their fake stress test.

The Federal Reserve System is fighting tooth and nail to prevent this disclosure, because if their $500 trillion dollars or so of derivatives were actually placed on their balance sheet, using the "market to market" rule, they would be shown to be bankrupt.

Some banks are now working to bring about the NESARA mission in hopes that the Prosperity funds would trickle into their banks, saving them from closing their doors, but most of the larger banks that are fighting the coming changes will soon be out of business. They are not informing their employees of the new regulation and thus will not be ready to operate under a gold banking charter.

Slowly, the illegal practices of the international financiers are coming to an end. One by one the mayor banking houses are imploding right before our eyes.

Their train wreck is occurring because these banks

are no longer allowed to use assets from the collateral account of the global debt Facility to backup their loans. This is why we are seeing their derivatives implode.

The banks have been illegally using the collateral account, as collateral for their gold backed derivatives, bullion certificates, and bonds sold to offshore domiciled corporations.

With the new Basel II rules in place these derivative assets have now become worthless garbage, resulting in the massive banking writ-downs you see today.

According to the *Office of International Treasury Control* this over-the-counter derivative market is worth about $3.3 quadrillion dollars; with J.P. Morgan leading the pack, with hundreds of trillion dollars of derivatives.

During the Clinton years, the banking 1:10 fractional reserve ratio was increased to 1:100. This easy money allowed anyone to get a home loan resulting in the housing sector boom.

Since many of these loans were made to risky low income households, the banks deferred their risk by selling their loan portfolios to investors, in a process known as Securitization. This occurs when mortgages are repackaged with other mortgages in a giant pool of liquidity, which are sold to investors on the global market.

These credit derivatives can then be repackaged and leveraged again at another 100:1 ratio, which is then repeated, over and over, until there is literally quadrillions of dollars of derivatives floating around in the world's bankrupt system.

When housing prices were going up, these derivatives were making fortunes for the banks' and the government's offshore accounts, allowing them to buy up assets all over the world with virtually free money.

When investors realized these derivatives contained toxic loans, they stopped their buying binge causing the credit market to seize up, which is why housing prices are in free fall.

Because no one wants to buy these toxic derivatives, the banks and the government are now in a panic to find other people's money to plug up the holes in the cracking dam.

Though some funds have been raised by selling military secrets to China, or through CIA drug running operations, this is nowhere near enough money to prop up a collapsing derivative market; so now the government is resorting to stealing the money, which is no credible way to run a country.

To put a stop to this criminal activity, in December, 2009, INTERPOL was given legal jurisdiction within the US, to hunt down and arrest crooked bankers.

April 4, 2008 marked the expiration of the 70 year bankruptcy agreement of the United States, beginning in 1938. Technically, the Bankruptcy began in 1933, but the Supreme Court did not enforce it until the United States became a legislative democracy in 1938.

The nations of the world, weary of the shenanigans of the Federal Reserve System, knew they had a limited time to foreclose on the United States before the corporate government could extend another 70 year extension of the Bankruptcy.

Without this protection, the government was now at the mercy of its creditors who were demanding reforms of the banking system, such as higher net capital requirements found under Basel II. If the United States failed to meet their demands, they would be cut off from the international markets.

So to raise the funds needed, in August, 2008, the US Government began shorting the derivative market causing stock and commodity prices to fall worldwide. But this $20 trillion dollars of wealth was not destroyed; instead, it was transferred into the government's off-shore pension fund accounts, of which $5 trillion dollars were moved back into the United States, to shore up a collapsing dollar.

Soon, this money will run out, leaving the option of either crashing the financial market, or once again destroying what little is left of our American economy, or by printing more money, leading to hyperinflation.

But the global family does not want to see a devaluated dollar, as 90% of all US dollars in circulation today are held by foreigners; and they have no desire to see their assets evaporate, so they have agreed to back all dollars, printed before September 2008, with gold stored in the Philippines; at the rate of 1.28 grams of gold per dollar.

This would serve to curb the inflationary activities of the Federal Reserve, and the assets of the hard working average American, but on the other hand, all derivatives would be valued at 1/3rd of 1%, which is their fair market value, forcing those who own this toxic trash into bankruptcy and finally out of business.

On September 30th, 2009, the fiscal year of the United States came to a close. Because of the precarious financial situation of the United States, and its derivative holdings, the Chinese government reversed its policy of accepting fiat money for repayment of the national debt, so instead, they will only accept gold and silver as lawful payment, as specified in Article 1, Section 10 of the United States Constitution.

To meet these new demands, the owners of the Federal Reserve System are scrambling to purchase enough gold and silver; but no one wants to sell them any.

While the Federal Reserve System is falling apart, Barry Sotero continues to block the NESARA deliveries. Even though he never invested any money in these programs, he demands a portion of these funds for himself.

In a pattern which mimics the Bush years, the Obama administration continues to make new daily attempts to steal the funds. But before he was even sworn into office, in December, 2008, Obama tried unsuccessfully to steal $400 billion dollars from the Prosperity funds, and demanded another $1 trillion dollars ransom for his deed.

A week before his inauguration, Saint Germain and the global family had confronted Obama about his actions. At that time, Obama agreed to go along with the NESARA mission, but soon after reversed his promise and has now solidified his alliance with the Bush/Clinton cabal.

"Our economy is badly weakened as a consequence of greed and irresponsibility on the part of some, but also our collective failure to make hard choices, and prepare the nation for a new age." — Obama.

In March, 2009, Obama tried once again to steal

over $200 trillion dollars of international funds from the Bank of International Settlements. This money was originally stolen by the Nazis from Holocaust victims and for the past 60 years had been earning interest in secret bank accounts.

When Obama was informed that the theft of international funds was an impeachable offense, he replied, *"You can't touch me. I'm above it."*

We knew where it was, so we took it.

As the largest holder of the national debt, the Chinese Government is now in control of the United States economy, its grain supply, and its communist President. Which is why Chinese President Hu doesn't want to see NESARA announced; otherwise it would negate this cushy arrangement.

In May, 2009, Obama sought help from the Chinese Government to hack into some of the trust accounts overseas. Had Obama been successful, China would have received a $4 trillion dollar payout for their cooperation. Lately, the White Knights located the money and it is now in a safe place.

This report is a ***specific transcript*** of portions of narrator and producer James Rink's three years of hard work entitled ***Change is on the Horizon*** — a YourTube Video uploaded on June 15, 2011 — about **NESARA**.

http://tinyurl.com/67whr8w

NESARA I

Continuing

Prosperity Programs & NESARA

Since the beginning of our known recorded history humans have used barter and exchange in society.

Since the earliest days of time, people have used items of value as a barter tool for goods and services.

The Money Changers have always sought to control the exchange system as one method of the enslavement of man. Take for example the story of Jesus driving the Money Changers out of the temple. The Money Changers required worshipers to exchange their gifts (of spices, wares and precious metals etc.) into a specific form of currency (the temple tax) for a fee.

Over the ages the Money Changers have been hard at work controlling the barter, or currency system that we know today as money.

The Money Changers have been working most diligently at perfecting the money changer concept. Today we know it as fractional reserve banking. To put it simply, based on a $1000 value of gold they issue $10,000 (or more) paper dollars or pounds. (for a ratio of 10 or even much more to 1).

The Money Changers charge the issuing government interest on every dollar or pound printed or created by effortless key strokes on a computer.

The current monetary system is the Money Changers on steroids! The primary examples of the fractional reserve predator's are The Bank of England and The Federal Reserve. These institutions are controlled not by the government, but by individuals, or the Money Changers themselves.

You are encouraged to learn more about this system of enslavement in order to prevent it from happening again.

Part of The Plan by the forces of Redemption is to break up this monopoly game of control. This is happening before your very eyes. The financial tsunami you are witnessing is the Money Changers' enslavement system collapsing under it's own weight. The system has become so corrupt it is unable to withstand the light of day.

Basel II and III banking protocols are being instituted which force the banks and financial institutions to open their crooked books to the light. The result is what you can read about in your news sources today — total bank failure. This is part of a grand design to release humanity from the strangle hold of a corrupt financial system designed to maintain total control. Just ponder for a moment on how money and the current form of barter affects every aspect of your life!

There are many elements to The Plan. One of those elements is NESARA and The Prosperity Programs.

The monetary Trust Fund of St. Germain was established in the 18th century. This trust fund was based upon precious metals and minerals (gold, silver, diamonds etc.). Because the funds were based upon these constant items of value, they were immune to the control of currency systems of the money changers of the day. The values of gold and precious minerals have only increased and recently have begun to sky rocket. Look at the value of gold today against the currency systems. There are also massive reserves of precious metals and minerals hidden away from the money changers in our Mother Earth. NESARA is the **National Economic Security and Reformation Act.**

The NESARA Act is actually part of a global plan. It is designed to dismantle the United States financial system that controls the de facto standard currency of the whole world.

When NESARA is announced and implemented the Prosperity Programs, Farm Claims, and other trusts will also be released.

The recipients include individuals and governments. Most of the recipients are unknown, as a form of protection from the Elite. The overall plan has been kept secret, as you will learn in your own research. This has been and continues to be a strategic element of the plan.

The Money Changers have been hard at work in preventing the enactment of the plan, as you will learn. When the funds are distributed some of the recipients will be required to disburse a certain percentage of their funds to others. They will be required to locate suitable persons that are willing to use the funds for the LOVE of mankind.

Eventually every man woman and child on Earth will benefit from the programs. The idea is to flood the world with so much prosperity that the pursuit of happiness will become the only goal for all mankind. Governments and individuals will no longer be able to use currency to control humanity.

Right now Patriot Workers are being encouraged to become involved and use their gifts to facilitate this Republic plan. We are being encouraged to use the Love and Light within us to come up with personal and government projects to insure the use of funds for the good of all mankind.

You are being asked to conceive of projects that you feel are worthy pursuits to help and educate all the people of the world. To help to restore the beauty and magnificence of the world. If you had unlimited resources what would you do?

You have been prepared for this mission, now is the time to get busy and make it happen. You are encouraged to ask for guidance, use your personal interests and skills to develop projects to help bring all of mankind into the Light. We have been told over and over that God is NOT going to do this FOR us.

There is not going to be a magical solution to all of the worlds problems. **We are the warriors of Light and Love! Now is the time to get to work.** Think about it. How did you think we were going to make a difference? This is but one part of the overall plan.

The elements of Love and Light are with you, encouraging you every step of the way. Listen to your heart and it will guide you upon your path. You will instinctively know what to do at the right time.

The collapse of the Dark Cabal is imminent! Your time to really shine has come.

Producer and Narrator James Rink

NESARA Now

We need NESARA, NOW! To stop the unlawful corporate US government from starting world war three. NESARA ends the unconstitutionality of the Federal Reserve Banking system.

NESARA stands for *National Economic Security and Reformation Act.*

The beginnings of this law took place in the early 1990's when banks began to illegally foreclose on framers homes. The "Live Aid" concerts was one of the fund raisers to helps these farmers. The farmers got together and when they realized what was going on they started a lawsuit against the government. In retaliation the Government sent the IRS against the lawyers. As a result the lawyers requested the assistance of military generals.

These generals would then sit in the court rooms to make sure the bribed judges would rule in favor of constitutional law. It was determined in these cases that not only were the banks illegally foreclosing on mortgages, but the money itself was worthless (the dollar has no precious metals supporting it).

Because the Constitution states that only gold and silver can be accepted forms of coinage/currency these judges ruled the Federal Reserve Banking system to be illegal and to be abolished. These trials went all the way up to the Supreme Court.

Years passed and the generals realized the government had no intentions to abolish the Fed. As result, the order was given to surround Congress and force members to sign NESARA into law under gunpoint. This happened on March 9, 2000.

Then under the gunpoint of elite Naval Seals and the Delta Force, on October 10, 2000, Bill Clinton signed this act into law. This was necessary because the Illuminati are in full control of our government. Also, the Clinton's where never lawfully elected. Ross Perot was lawfully elected to be our president, at that time.

NESARA requires all members of Congress and the President to resign, and new elections to take place. It disbands the Federal Reserve Bank, and replaces it with currency of the US Treasury, backed by precious metals.

All debt will be zeroed out to make way for the new currency. The IRS will be replaced with a national sales tax.

NESARA releases all suppressed technologies such as free energy devices which can clean up all pollution and cure all diseases, even old age. It also begins refunds of stolen monies to be given out in the form of debit cards. Every American citizen, over the age of 21, will receive $100,000 a month for 11 years, as compensation for all the evil perpetrated against them by the American Federal Empire.

Folks, no microchipping will be required for this refund, unlike some would have you believe. According to a secret FBI, CIA, and NSA, study one out of ten Americans have already been chipped by the grays. This research, known as the Roper Report, was sent to over 100,000 psychologist's.

Those involved with the Christian cult refuse to look at the fact, that we are already chipped; many of whom include them!

Now understand, the Fed is not a Federal Bank, it is privately owned bank, controlled by the most wealthy families of the world. These people are like leeches sucking off the lifeblood of the world's poor. They include 300 of the world's wealthiest banking families, such as the Windsor's, Lazard brothers, Rothschild's, and Rockefeller's. Even the Bush family has a piece of the pie; they own the Carlyle Group which is worth $370 trillion dollars. All money paid into the IRS, is deposited into the Fed, and distributed to them.

63% to the Crown of England and various banking families; 27% to the worlds 300 most wealthiest illuminati families; and 10% to the Employees of the IRS.

(The Crown is a one square mile Country located in the central part of London, owned by the House of Windsor, the British Monarchy).

NESARA will pay them off so they will give up their monopolies.

All money paid into the IRS has gone to the Federal Reserve Bank since 1913. It is estimated that the Fed has stolen over $500 trillion dollars, less interest and inflation, over this period of time. None of this money has financed the U.S. government as we know it today.

Money is raised via CAFR (from the Comprehensive Annual Financial Reports), CIA Drug Trafficking, and Arms Trafficking, as well.

The Constitutional government that we believe in is no more. It was bankrupted in 1933. That's what the New Deal was all about. In 1933 the Constitutional government was dismantled, and the Zionist NEW World Order Government was formed as a new corporation called THE UNITED STATES OF AMERICA.

Its property included all lands, property, and even "we the people". They are using us as their chattel. This is why we have Social Security numbers, and why the government can deduct money from our wages for the IRS. Today, this shadow government is running the show, using its easy money to finance secret black Ops involving ET's, and much more.

The amount of wealth the Illuminati have stolen is so astonishingly huge, that it's incomprehensible to the average man. The worlds total GDP is estimated to be about $30 trillion dollars, annually. However, the total wealth of the Illuminati is in excess of Tens of quadrillion dollars!

But, even so, they are not the wealthiest group on the planet. The wealthiest person is Saint Germain. His trust fund was set up over 280 years ago, in 1729.

These funds were meant to be released in the year 2000 for benevolent purposes.

Today that fund is now worth $1 quatrodecillion or 1,000,000,000,000,000,000,000,000,000,000,000,000,000,000,000. dollars. That's enough money to buy a gold cube the size of the orbit of Saturn. So *astronomical,* the average person will not be able to believe it. His secret money making techniques shall remain secret for now. However, their is no secret on how the illuminati have made their money.

Their methods include:

a. Ripping of third world nations via the International Monetary Fund

b. Fractional Reserve Banking

c. Fiat currency

d. Drug Trafficking

e. Oil

f. Backward engineered UFO technology for sale in the public sector

g. Arms Trafficking

h. Prostitution

Much of the funding for NESARA began 100 years ago. The children of robber barons began to put aside some of their family's money into secret trust funds. This money, along with the Saint Germain Trust was meant to be released into the world, to make right some of the wrongs of their parents. This money will be used to buy out all oil companies, energy conglomerates, banks, pharmaceutical cartels, and zero out all debt.

NESARA literally ushers in the Golden Age of humanity!

The whore, media, refuses to publish this knowledge because the Supreme Court placed gag order on any media, or government, personnel, with the threat of death if they talk.

This is why Alex Jones and Wikipedia will not discuss this information. In addition the associated press and Reuters have been bought off by the Rothschild family, since 1901. 85% of all news networks are owned by only 5 corporations. Do you really think Rupert Murdoch is going to tell you the truth?

We live in an Orwellian state. Wake Up!

NESARA was planned to be announced on September 11, 2001, at 10:00 A.M. Just before the announcement, Bush Sr. ordered the destruction of the World Trade Center, to block to distribution of the NESARA refunds, and kill the Pro NESARA military supporters located in the White Knights HQ of the Pentagon.

This effectively destroyed the first attempt to bring this country back to Constitutional law. Bush Jr, our then president was just a puppet, he was so cloned and chipped he probably had no clue what's really going on at the time.

The destruction on 9/11 served to start an unjust war with Afghanistan and IRAQ. This war was necessary because, since 1980's, OPEC has effectively forced the world to trade for all barrels of oil in Federal Reserve Notes.

This means that our money is backed by Oil. This is why no free energy technologies will be released until the Federal Reserve Bank is abolished. Our money supply is a ticking time bomb waiting to be set off. The Illuminati need this war to force "Rouge" nations to continue using worthless Federal Reserve notes.

Sadam was trading oil for Euro's, and Afghanistan refused to let Halliburtion build a pipeline, across its land to the Caspian sea, at the price Halliburton wanted. Enron's, Ken Lay, was murdered because he threatened the Bush family about going public about these secret dealings.

The Illuminati are using secret bank accounts in the Bahamas and Cayman Islands to prop up the stock market. Once the money stops flowing, expect a total melt down. Unless NESARA happens.

People who are anti-NESARA are like the same folks in the times of Noah, mockers and scoffers of truth. Did not the scriptures say, as it is in the days of Noah so it will be in the last days? Also, "even the very elect would be deceived."

The elect are not those phony unelected officials who run the government, nor are they those who are involved with the Christian cult. The elect are the 144,000 who have come back, to return this planet back to the light.

People like those who run http://www.Quatloos.com (CIA front) , and CIA agent, Sherry Shriner, will end up in the ash heap of history.

Now you know.
So be it.
- James

Summation

NESARA will bring most of the world's people increased prosperity, liberty, peace, and more knowledge, which will enable them to flourish.

This compilation is intended to act as a reference to what can be expected when the announcement is finally broadcast on radio and TV.

Times will be different. We will be taking a quantum leap into a brave, new world.

There will be a complete restructuring of society, and especially the business world. There will be those who cannot or will not accept the new conditions and form a separate society that will not be long-lived.

For the others, this is the beginning of the Golden Age. A time of Peace, not War, when the Lion shall lie down with the Lamb.

We were told that, because of the long delay in implementing NESARA, post-NESARA activities would be greatly speeded up. The worldwide program should have already been in place. There have been delays in getting as many as possible of the Dark Forces to join the Light, before the announcement is made. But this too is just the beginning of the Golden Age: there is much more to come.

What is being 'speeded up'? One can only conjecture. One of the principal benefits, to be implemented within one to four months after the implementation of NESARA, is the realignment of prices world-wide, so most likely that would be one benefit brought forward for implementation.

One of the most amazing improvements that will roll out from NESARA, and across the world, is that all people will eventually have the same rights that Americans have, when NESARA restores the American Constitution and the Bill of Rights to the law of the land (Common Law rather than statute law). 180 countries have signed treaties to implement NESARA.

There have been many prophecies of catastrophic earth changes about this current time. We are assured that times have changed and this will not happen to the extent originally foreseen; because mankind has made great strides in spiritual advancement.

Prophecy is always seen from the point of view of the time when the prophecy is made, but subsequent events can, and often do, alter these foreseen events. This is not a "failed prophecy": the nature of prophecy must be understood.

1
Cost of Living &
Other Financial Matters

in several months of the announcement, there will be a 90% reduction in the prices of ALL services and goods, to counter inflation and bring us back to the pricing of the 'fifties.

All countries involved have already made arrangements to implement that change, industry-wide. Prices will then be tied to the price of gold.

An equivalent reduction in salaries will not take place until a month or so after the re-pricing of goods and services. This will give employees one month or more of bonus spending power!

Remember that cash (in hand or at the bank) is NOT devalued. That means that if you have $50,000 right now and wish to buy a new home costing $250,000, the new price of the home would be just $25,000, so instead of making a down-payment you could purchase it outright and still have $25,000 left over - as the value of money held right now is NOT devalued. There would also be NO tax on the purchase.

The same would apply to a new motor vehicle.

A top of the line vehicle might cost $50,000 right now, but only $5,000 after re-pricing, leaving one enough left over to enjoy life in that paid-in-full vehicle.

The merchant however might think, that is just not feasible - I cannot afford to sell a vehicle for $5,000 when I paid (the wholesale equivalent of) $50,000 to put it into my showroom!

Yes, you can: the merchant will not lose anything: whether your product is motor vehicles or groceries, at the time of re-pricing you take inventory at the current price, deduct the inventory value at the new price, then the difference (which would appear to be a loss) is claimed back through Treasury - this is the assumed process, as no information has as yet been made public.

Just 3% of the world's population currently control 95% of the world's wealth, but NESARA will be a great leveller - *"the meek shall inherit the Earth"*.

NESARA will benefit the average person most of all: wealth will be much more evenly distributed - are you ready for such responsibility?

It may take a decade for complete elimination of poverty and hunger and for a while only new spacecraft will be available for the transportation and disbursement of food and other material to places where it is needed. Plans have already been made.

There will be a substantial increase in the amount paid out as various pensions, disability allowances, social security payments and family support payments. The standard of living for almost everyone will therefore be greatly improved. These payments will continue until replaced by amounts paid out as compensation for past government and bank fraud, begin. There will be no need for anyone having to live at the "survival level."

The payments paid out as compensation for past government and bank fraud are stated to be $75,000 monthly for 12 years, or until $10 million dollars is reached. Advances on that sum might be made for special purposes.

Tremendous wealth will also be created through the "Prosperity Programs" as billions of dollars are distributed to individuals on 'gifting lists'. In many cases this will create a personal security problem as news of the sudden prosperity of one's neighbour leaks out. One of the many suggestions as to how to handle this is quite simply, to MOVE - get out of the neighborhood and start your life afresh somewhere else. Keep the information to yourself if possible, and also from relatives - unless you relish them laying siege to your door.

This sudden wealth will have a significant beneficial effect on the world economy: people have more money to spend, and spend they will, particularly on high-priced items.

Having riches beyond compare does not necessarily mean having an easy life: it takes much thought, discipline and responsibility of action. Some opponents of NESARA protest that it will give people too much money to spend and create irresponsibility.

Responsibility, or irresponsibility, already exists - it will not be created by NESARA. It will be a continuation of tests, but in a different vein. It is immeasurably better than servitude, which has been the fate of too many for too long.

Acquiring great riches must be one of the most exacting tests we can undergo. Are *you* ready??

The fact that it is backed by precious metals will also increase the value of the dollar, which right now is a worthless piece of paper, printed ad lib by the (operators/directors of) the Central Bank.

Some people, such as IRS employees, will find that their jobs no longer exist or their income is decreased by the announcement of NESARA.

All people who can show that their income has been reduced by NESARA will be eligible to apply for generous financial allotments which will carry them through until they have new income sources.

But the delay in implementation has reduced some of the benefits. Getting prices back to the level of the 'fifties is now highly unlikely. Manufacturers in most fields, knowing about the impending re-pricing, have significantly increased their retail prices. As much as 50 - 100%, or more, in some cases. Food prices have also soared.

And in Britain, for example, a townhouse which sold for £4,200 in 1964 sold for £6,200 in 1969; for £12,000 in the mid-'70s, and now sells for over £100,000.

2
Business

With bank debt forgiveness comes also the elimination of the NATIONAL DEBT (or at least 90% of it) - a tremendous boon to most countries in the world. These countries will no longer be ruled by a foreign power.

Except for businesses producing non-essential goods or services, the income tax will be eliminated and the new sales tax, *which will go to the government for the first time,* will not apply, reducing time spent on this operation.

Humanitarian and environmental projects will constitute the greatest benefits that NESARA brings to this world. This new era will bring about much redeployment of labor forces: some industries will close down and others rise up.

There will also be new kinds of corporations which we can use after NESARA is announced. It will be easier to hold the people who make decisions for corporations accountable for their actions.

After the announcement of NESARA, corporations will have a number of months to make the changes required. There will be public education about the changes required and how the changes are to be made. Corporations will have plenty of time to make these changes. In all areas of commerce changes will come in, and the large conglomerates will be made into more easily managed units. New methods of production will be totally efficient without being wasteful, and pollution will become a thing of the past.

Financial planners and everyone else will have to forget most of what they now know. Some well-known financial management experts have been educated about NESARA and are prepared to assist with the educational process after the announcement.

INCORPORATION:

Businesses will operate from a service charter rather than a business charter to provide services and produce goods. There will be no requirement to obtain permission from the State to operate a business. Non-profit corporations, as such, will disappear - they exist only for tax purposes and government control, neither of which will continue.

Requirements will be more like a certificate stating the purpose, the social and financial responsibilities through a guiding (not controlling) body. There will be no "charities" as such, for the same reason. More information will be made available after the NESARA announcement and the return to Common Law.

Banks will be quite different, to all other operations. There will be no more shareholders. The banking system is a distinct part of the Divine Plan for Earth in this place and time as a social facilita-tion device, and will not be allowed to return to being a medium of control.

PRICE CHANGES:

To defeat inflation, prices will be reduced 90% about 3 to nine month after the announcement of NESARA.

After, say, 30 days, wages and salaries will likewise be reduced. This gives employees several months with extremely low prices, before a balance is again struck.

When NESARA is announced, the fact that the new U.S. Treasury currency is backed by precious metals will have an impact on international trade. Companies in other countries which sell products to the U.S. will need to adjust their billing records for the products that have been sold to be distributed through U.S. locations. After NESARA's announce-ment the U.S. economy will be based on the new U.S. Treasury currency.

Currently, companies such as Toyota and Honda, which make their products in other countries and distribute the products in the U.S., have contracted to sell their cars to U.S. companies for specific prices that are based on the U.S. Federal Reserve currency which is not backed by precious metals.

However, when the new U.S. Treasury currency is announced these foreign companies will have to change the amounts they are charging the U.S. companies to reflect the fact that the U.S. companies will now be paying for imported products with new U.S. Treasury currency which is more valuable than the Federal Reserve notes.

There are three other major currencies which are supposed to announce their own new banking and currency improvements within days after NESARA is announced.

The European Central Bank is supposed to announce the Euro as backed by precious metals, within three business days of NESARA's announcement.

The British banking system is supposed to announce that the British Pound is backed by precious metals, within one week of NESARA's announcement.

The Japanese banking system is supposed to

announce that the Japanese Yen is backed by precious metals, within one week of NESARA's announce-ment.

There are some other countries which will announce that their currencies also are backed by precious metals, soon after NESARA's announce-ment.

The currency markets, stock markets, and commodity markets will be closed immediately for several days after NESARA is announced.

Many of the fundamental economic principles of our world economy will change after officials of these major banking and currency systems announce that they are backed by precious metals.

Therefore considerable re-education will be required and broadcast by television and radio and covered in newspapers which will inform us of new economic principles based on the fact that major banking systems and currencies are backed by precious metals.

Greenspan compiled 30 hours of video-taped education which will be broadcast to help us understand our world's new economic principles.

In these ways, NESARA's announcement starts a ripple effect around the world. It's important that these other countries announce their improved banking and currency systems very soon after NESARA's announce-ment as part of keeping the world economy stable.

The stock markets will cease business and monies will be refunded. No more gambling! Did you think they actually served a useful purpose?

BUSINESS OPPORTUNITIES:

NESARA will present the most dramatic change in business and manufacturing opportunities worldwide that the world has ever seen - even greater than the Industrial Revolution.

There will no longer be any demand for many services and products, initially causing unemploy-ment, but this will be more than compensated for by the new opportunities presented and the increase in demand for existing natural products.

One example will be the replacement of noisy, polluting commercial jet aircraft by silent, pollution-free shuttlecraft ("flying saucers"), and small spaceports replacing today's airports with their runways taking up miles of what could otherwise be fertile land.

Scrap merchants will have a hey-day as the amount of scrap metal due to come on the market will be astronomical - not just from the military but from many other sectors as well.

Automotive manufacturers have already planned the mass introduction of electric vehicles. There will undoubtedly be many new manufacturers of conversion kits to eliminate fossil fuel usage.

This will extend to almost all industries that use energy in one way or another, and of course the utilities will be affected almost immediately.

No more nuclear power plants, no more coal-burning, polluting iron-horses, all consigned to museums. It opens up more opportunities than it eliminates through job losses in the soon-to-become-extinct industries mentioned.

Most people do not realise how much their world has been controlled by a select group - who have now lost their power. This means that to maintain your <u>health</u> you are no longer required to use pharmaceutical drugs, but you - as well as hospitals and clinics - will be able to use much less expensive - and more effective - natural remedies.

Free energy will replace 'natural resources' such as petroleum products, and the technology that has been suppressed for decades will spawn immense opportunities for factories producing all kinds of engines, using cosmic energy (no more gas tanks). Such industries will require the distribution and ancillary services required by all industries.

Will it happen overnight?

Unlikely, but welcome to a completely new world. All fossil-fuelled vehicles will not be able to run and replacement will be a matter of urgency. Those in a position to do so should start planning production now! Funds will be available.

Here is how Abraham Lincoln summed it up: ***"There will be an upheaval such as this continent has never before witnessed. People will be uprooted, businesses will crumble, empires will fall, and all for the good. Let the light shine on the good, and let the fearful run and hide.***

3
Religion

The NESARA Year should be an historic year in many ways. The Church itself could be shaken to its very core. By "Church", understand *ALL* religions, not just Christianity.

This is alleged to be the year of the Second Coming. The Second Coming has been traditionally preached from the pulpit of most churches - but which the preachers themselves probably hope never occurs in their own lifetime!

The 2,000 years are up. There are two matters often overlooked in church circles - that the Man of Galilee said that He would return, and that he would have a new name when He returned. His new name is alleged to be 'Sananda', but he will answer to any appellation used. It is the thought that is heard.

2,000 years ago he had a fore-runner, John the Baptist. This time there will *also* be a fore-runner - but another shock is in store for the male ego: this is the *Age of Femininity*, and his forerunner, *this time,* will be female!

This will be a body blow to those churches who have kept women downtrodden for so long. Time for a fresh outlook on life!

Each religion will have its own "Messiah" return, with two messengers. So Mohammed and Buddha will also be back.

So what strikes such fear into the heart of the Church? Should they not be rejoicing? If they are *NOT* rejoicing, then surely something must be wrong? Perhaps they have hidden some truths from us, and fear that these will now be disclosed?

Zion means "America", so he will come first to the North American continent, then he will travel on to Jerusalem, to help iron out the differences between Arab and the Jew.

One of the messages to the Church will be that we should work together, as we all are ONE ... and here are some truths that have been overlooked, even suppressed.

Those churches which do not comply will wither away and disappear from the scene.

Nostradamus stated that *"**wise people from western and eastern tradition will meet at common ground to help develop philosophies that will progress towards world peace.**"*

Most of the other prophecies of old, biblical or otherwise, no longer apply as the path taken by planet Earth and its inhabitants has drastically changed with the unexpectedly great increase in spiritual understanding, especially in the last few years.

The "new" doctrines to be followed are not actually "new" - they have just been conveniently hidden under the table as unsuitable for an organization which has traditionally sought to control the people.

The most important being that of "reincarnation."

There will be much consternation at first. The people (who are much more informed these days, thanks particularly to the Internet) will start asking their spiritual leaders to explain why they have been misled for so long, so it behooves the clergy to prepare answers as quickly as possible, thereby ensuring that they will still have a livelihood in this 'business'.

The churches will quickly empty unless the members and adherents are given authoritative advice. But there is evidence that there is a warming in ecclesiastical circles that should lead to a more open dialogue and a working together for the betterment of all. The skies of the future are clearing.

The winds of change will blow, and they will strike the pastors as well as the congregations.

NESARA I

4
Courts, Judges & Lawyers of the Future

It had been hinted at before, but Abraham Lincoln once stated how law courts of the future would be run.

There will be NO LAWYERS!

Well, think of the effect on the State of California, where it is claimed that 10% of its citizens are lawyers or attorneys!

It's goodbye to corrupt judges and lawyers - and few will be sorry to see them go.

In their place should be TEN JUST MEN in every community, elected by the residents of that community, who would hear complaints and recommend presentments to Grand Juries.

This fits in well with the return to Common Law.

Of course it does not mean that those currently practising law or administering justice cannot become one of these selected TEN. There are many admirable judges and lawyers, but too often they have been squeezed out of practice by less honourable gentlemen.

These new courts will be kept busy for a long time to come. But one more thing should be said. With the return to common or constitutional law, all *statute laws* will be revoked.

Gradually there will be an increase in telepathic ability. Eventually, nothing will be hidden that will not be known, and lawlessness will altogether cease.

Sounds Utopian, but it will bo so sooner than people think. Not necessarily overnight, but in time for many to think things over, and adjust their attitudes in life.

Telepathy is perhaps best explained by considering the ability of an animal to sense fear in man, even when nothing is said and no actions are taken. Or when you meet someone for the first time, and for no apparent reason you either like them, or dislike them intensely. We call it a sixth sense, but in reality it is telepathy: thought transfer between individuals. Some are born with this ability, others must learn it and it is now being taught widely for the first time.

COMMON LAW

Reports indicate that the World Court sent ouinstructions to dozens of leaders of countries ordering them to adopt Common Law within a month after NESARA's announcement.

The adoption of Common Law worldwide is important to maintaining stability, and smooth transitions, as NESARA's international impact on banking and legal systems rolls out across the world.

Interestingly, a few years ago the French Finance Minister was seen and heard on a television network saying that the entire world would be experiencing prosperity under Common Law. This was one of those hints about NESARA which frequently occurred; but was not repeated in American news.

It is estimated that there are more than one billion laws on the books in the United States. In the current statutory legal system if you break one of these one billion laws but don't know it, that's not a legal defense.

How could anyone reasonably be expected to know all one billion laws in the U.S.?

Obviously, the current U.S. legal system is overloaded with laws and unreasonable assumptions.

When NESARA is announced, every court will be immediately closed and all judges will be required to attend training in Constitutional Law.

All law enforcement personnel and others connected with law enforcement will also be required to attend Constitutional Law training. The basics of Constitutional Law are things all of us should be able to understand fairly easily, and public education will be provided to us in the media, and in other ways.

The change to Constitutional Law is expected to occur about one month after NESARA's announcement.

Pending Cases will have to be resubmitted under Constitutional Law. People in prison for victimless crimes, things like income tax issues which are not crimes under Constitutional Law, will be released from prison within 60 days after NESARA's announcement.

The 1993, the United States Supreme Court, in rulings which are embodied in NESARA, found that the so-called "income" tax amendment to the Constitution (Amendment 16) had never been ratified. Fraudulent paperwork was used to back up the federal government's false contention that the income tax amendment had been ratified by the required number of states.

The restoration of Constitutional Law requires that all judges, law enforcement, and others, *MUST* attend educational seminars and learn about Constitutional Law. All courts will be closed for at least one month while these Constitutional Law seminars are being conducted.

Any court cases in process will have to be re-filed using Constitutional Law foundations; many cases now clogging up the court systems will no longer be valid court cases under Constitutional Law.

In addition, many people who have been imprisoned under unconstitutional laws such as income tax laws, will be released from prison within weeks after NESARA is announced.

There will also be educational seminars on television regarding Constitutional Law which is based on Common Law and we all will be learning about this.

5
Comminications

Our current communications systems, regardless of how 'hi-tech' they advertise themselves to be, are still primitive.

It has been said that the Internet system - one of the most educational and informative tools of the current age - will be no longer required, as mankind will have more advanced means of communicating. We think it will be around for a while yet nevertheless.

When we really understand how to harness light and sound waves, computers will no longer be necessary.

Those who have taught the Illuminati in the past the 'secrets' of higher technology will now teach us to put this knowledge to better use. It will probably be a few years yet before we reach this stage - closer to 2012.

Inter-galactic communication will captivate the attention of Earth-dwellers for some time to come.

By early 2005 it had been reported that 'Faster-Than-Light' communication devices had been produced for communications with extra-terrestrial sources. It was also stated that telepathy would become widespread, not just for ET-communications but for communication between humans as a whole ..... a very interesting scenario, as then, no thought could be kept secret!

NESARA I

6
21st Century Residential Construction

While reading the works of Edgar Cayce we noted that he had stated that future homes would be made out of a combination of metal and glass. We are still looking for the introduction of such a material: it has been hinted at on occasion, but no proof of its existence has been traced as of yet.

Many new applications involving concrete have been either marketed or await production financing, but concrete itself is *not* a suitable environment for human beings. The 'concrete jungle' is what we have been used to for decades and it has been recognised for quite some time now as an unhealthy environment - but no practical replacement has as yet been put into use.

Older buildings were made of stone or brick. Both these materials make comfortable residences, although in some climates they would require extra heating in winter to maintain a comfortable environment. In regions with a high rainfall, stone tends to grey quickly (as evidenced in older cities) and requires waterproofing.

Why do we have the desire to get away from built-up areas? We jump in the car and go off into the countryside. The buildings that are often in these concreted areas, including roads and walkways, are not conducive to creating the peaceful atmosphere that one instinctively seeks. The energies of people and all manner of activities and noise leave their marks for a long time, and are trapped there until they finally diminish. What concrete jungles do is to stifle the natural energies from Mother Earth, and disturb what otherwise should be a pleasant and healthy environment. The energies become ugly and discordant and can reach the point of becoming unhealthy in the worst scenario.

In the future each building will be self-sufficient and require no outside supplies and all will be self contained.

There are some systems which can be introduced right now which can contribute to better living, stronger construction or quicker turnaround time:

1. The laws of structural engineering have been re-written, according to the Engineering Department of the University of Alberta, the University of BC and a similar institute in Japan, by the concept of the *Wolfhook*, a component locking device, patented by Wolf Creative Designs which adds immense strength to the post and beam framework of any building.

2. The new trade name for this advanced technology is "Hook&Build ™ Building Systems"

One other alternative in building construction would be a return to dowels rather than nails, which likewise binds the components together, although shrinkage might play a factor here and cause looseness over time. This would also alter the emphasis on trades within the construction industry.

3. These two concepts should result in a building structure unaffected by the most intense weather patterns, and which should remain intact even during seismic disturbances.

Reusable forms for the construction, in jigsaw fashion, of floors in high-rise buildings.

Back in the '50s, in Western Germany, a concrete foamed block was marketed which allowed houses to be built in a couple of days. The standard construction block was 1 meter long and could easily be picked up by one man. An attempt was made to introduce it into the market, but it fell foul of the building code, which other manufacturers in collusion with government made sure was not changed.

Of course, this was also made partly of concrete so it was not an ideal construction material.

One other aspect still not recognised - and it would be very inconvenient to recognise it - is that human beings should NOT live one on top of another, such as happens in high-rise buildings.

There is a lack of understanding of life, deliberately omitted from our education systems (they are directed more to the 'dumbing-down' of future generations rather than instilling them with knowledge), which results in the essentials of living being largely ignored by the construction industry.

A human being constantly emits energy in the form of frequencies, which radiate mainly vertically, both up and down (radially to some extent also - about one meter in general).

These emanations can consist of very negative energies - anger, jealousy, outbursts of rage, or even more serious emotions and actions, which then travel vertically and are picked up by everyone in its path. That means that in a 30-story-building, if you live on the 20th floor, you have the energies of 19 families below you and ten families above you to contend with.

So these great views from the penthouse come with

some real disadvantages.

High-rises allow a much higher population density, but at a cost to liveability.

The townhouse may offer the best solution for downtown living - unless one has noisy neighbours. It is always difficult to know just how much noise the walls will absorb and how much residual, unwelcome noise will come through to you. The only real alternative left is the free-standing dwelling, which could be the ultimate in living, but involves quite a bit more work on the individual's part to maintain to acceptable standards, and eats up 'valuable' urban space.

Living in the country does not present the same problems, but can we all live in the country? In this computer age, it has been suggested that this is quite a possibility. Working from home however poses one major social problem: lack of regular interaction with one's fellow workers or peers.

Living in communities has been a subject of discussion for decades. Originally it inferred communal living, which was definitely not for everyone, but that is not the case today. Even a small town or village is essentially a community, although it may lack the bonds that a new, intentional community can achieve.

7
Education

One of the greatest tasks facing us will be the implementation of a real education system - what we have now has little in common with what might be called 'education': it is a system for the 'dumbing-down' of the up-coming generations. It has been in place so long, and been so effective, that the problem is now a very serious one.

We have been deprived of the knowledge that should have been our birthright, therefore our understanding has been limited. This is the way that people are kept in ignorance - indeed, in slavery - without even realising it.

When you have teachers who themselves have not been taught, or who are not permitted to pass on the real knowledge which they have been taught, it is the teachers who must receive priority in re-training. We should have teachers who are competent to teach in the subjects allocated to them.

Visit a bookstore and you will see children's books classified according to age. This system is completely out-of-date: for children one-year old you might have to look in the '10-year old' section.

No wonder so many parents have taken to home-schooling. And the attitude of 'government' to home-schooling clearly indicates that they do not wish to see children properly educated.

And the textbooks which teachers are forced to use? - a good bonfire would be the best place for them. This means that we need new writers, who will compile proper textbooks for the education of children from kindergarten through to high school and beyond.

Perhaps some really old books can be found for reprinting, but they would have to be decades old. This will keep the publishing business going for some time. And the textbooks will not be changed every year: if the textbook is right for any purpose to start with, then it should be retained on a permanent basis, until something superior is made available.

Textbooks should be in truth - not dictated by New World Order psychologists and spin-doctors.

There will be a tremendous opening for the authoring of new textbooks exposing the truth rather than man-manufactured tales, or misleading so-called 'scientifically-proven' statements. Physics, for instance, will return to 'Walter Russell' physics and Nicola Tesla's work will receive full recognition. Even History must be rewritten.

A report from the National Association of Teachers of English in Britain states that there are plans to eliminate "English Literature" from final exams (A-levels) there, causing an uproar amongst those who recognise the dangers of such a loss. An elitist plot, it is called, preventing students from being acquainted with the real English language, and substituting the 'language of today's media' .....

Claire Fox, of the *Institute of Ideas* and a former English teacher, pointed out: "If you learn to read literature with a degree of sophistication, then that should rub off on you and help develop your writing ability."

Education should be completely freed up to at least tertiary level, Even tertiary level education should be free to those capable of utilising higher knowledge up to and including graduate level.

Family income has deteriorated to the extent that in most cases a mother needs to work, thus holding down two jobs. The women will begin to revolt, demanding higher wages for their husbands, so that they may remain at home and educate their children.

When the word "Educate" replaces "Raise" or "Rear", there will be an *onrush* for women to return home.

To educate a child is to teach it manners, and honesty, and dependability, and control of the will. This is done before the child is seven years of age. This will be stressed in many teachings by many leaders and Masters.

Pupils' lack of social skills leading to chaos

Too many children are not taught basic social standards by their parents, leading to classroom indiscipline, a teachers' leader claimed yesterday.

David Hart, the general secretary of the *National Association of Head Teachers* (NAHT), said the standard of behaviour in schools was decreasing because parents were not teaching even things such as toilet-training or how to use knives and forks.

In his last speech before he retires, Mr Hart told the NAHT's annual conference that the idea of "parent power" could backfire. He warned against allowing irresponsible parents to get even more power.

He said teaching staff were having to waste time teaching basics that should be taught in the home.

"By far and away the greatest problem is the number of pupils who lack basic social standards," he said. "They are not toilet-trained. They don't know how to use a knife and fork - that means that the teachers and support staff have got to spend their time sorting them out so that they are ready to be educated."

He said the negative effect of such children was passed on to other pupils, whose behaviour then deteriorates.

Delegates, who gave him a standing ovation, also heard him launch into an attack on parents who use verbal and physical threats, abuse, foul language, harassment and bullying when dealing with headteachers and their staff.

"And, by the way, giving more power to those parents who lack responsibility is like putting an alcoholic in charge of a bar," he said, in a reference aimed at the English education secretary, Ruth Kelly, who has said she wants to give parents more power in the classroom.

The problem of discipline has been a particular problem in schools in Scotland. Last week, Bill McGregor, the general secretary of the Headteachers Association Scotland, called on local authorities to use anti-social behaviour orders to protect teachers. He said that, if necessary, there should be an exclusion zone around school grounds for certain particularly violent pupils.

The most recent statistics, published more than a year ago, suggested that, on average, a teacher was attacked in Scotland every 12 minutes, and that the number of physical and verbal assaults on teachers and auxiliary staff had risen nine-fold in five years.

Last night, Ronnie Smith, the general secretary of the Education Institute of Scotland, said that a co-ordinated response to the problems of violence in schools was needed, involving teachers, parents, police and councils. He said: "All bad behaviour in society, whether it be the type you see on street corners on a Saturday night or the violence you see at some football matches, is brought into schools.

"We need to try to tackle anti-social behaviour in a co-ordinated way. Not just the schools, not just the parents and not just the police - we need to all have a set of standards that are acceptable to everyone and we need to all try to make them work."

Although he agreed with some of what Mr Hart said, he added that it was "obvious he is retiring" Mr Smith went on: "There are lots of kids that do not behave badly in schools. But the way they behave is often connected to home circumstances, be it difficult family circumstances or parents that do not instil the standards and behaviours that they should.

"The important thing for parents should not be how much power they have over the school. It is how much they take an interest in their children's education and work with the school."

Once NESARA has been announced we would like to get in touch with teachers and textbook writers, willing to assist in rebuilding the education system.

NESARA I

8
Government

Future governments will not consist of politicians, who have their own agenda (or the agenda of those businesses financing them) but rather scientists, researchers and administrators - professionals in their field, which will bring stability and accountability back to government. Representatives will be chosen for their wisdom, experience and spiritual understanding. Those with ulterior motives will be known, and there will be no place for them in the administrative organizations.

Political parties will be a thing of the past. Representatives will represent the people rather than the party.

Did you know that politicians must sign an agreement to vote as the party dictates rather than the people they 'represent'?

This was confirmed in a court of law in Alberta, Canada, many years ago, when an individual was elected on his promise to oppose the proposed new G.S.T. (sales tax), but when he got to Ottawa he voted *in favour* of it. The people took him to court - and THEY lost!

A signed piece of paper always takes precedence over verbal promises when it comes to a court of law.

The very word *'politician'* has a criminal ring to it these days. Few voice their own opinions. It is said that members of the US House of Congress each received two million dollars to support one group in Congress.

British PM Tony Blair is said to have received

personally $6 billion to side with President Bush in his war against Iraq. It has always been said that *Money talks .....*

The Bush Administration bribed Turkey and other countries to get their support in the U.N. for invading Iraq, and also threatened to withdraw foreign aid and impose other penalties if they didn't. *(The $26 billion bribe failed to persuade the Turkish parliament.)*

So how does a government keep its people from rebelling? Bear in mind the **four "Pillars of Control"** - **Fear**, **Guilt**, **Ignorance** and **Poverty**.

The Church is the principal tool as it covers all four.

Fear: Fear of God, rather than God's love and care for all mankind;

Guilt: ...born into sin;

Ignorance: suppression of knowledge and the promotion of disinformation;

Poverty: ...tithing, and many other demands for monies, to support the activities of the church.

All the false controls on planet Earth originated from a higher race ("the gods") who kept their knowledge to themselves and maintained the human races as their slaves. There were actually five races, distinguished still today by their color.

The Illuminati (those with knowledge) diversified into several fields, each with complete control over the people. Royalty was one branch; the Church was another; and the International Bankers were probably the most active.

The latter knew (as Meyer Rothschild once stated publicly) that if you control the purse strings of a nation, it does not matter which politicians or parties are in power.

Money is their principal tool, combined with interest.

Money itself has no value - banks are the only institutions which do not practise double-entry book-keeping as there is no other side to take into account - money is manufactured from nothing; and most of it today is "electronic." And it is constantly multiplied by unpayable interest - quite often compound interest - and fractional reserve expansion.

Mind Control

The Church keeps you in slavery by inviting you to become saved.

Wars are advanced for business reasons, by calling the soldiers peace-keepers. When you own the munitions factories, how else do you get customers?

The Government has used the terrorist threat for its own ends; create fear, and persuade the people to ask for more government controls.

The Bankers steal your money by instituting the income tax to finance the programs of your government - who receive not a penny from it: it is paid to the international banking families through the Federal Reserve Bank.

Politics has always been a hotbed of corruption, and it takes a strong person not to be tempted by the easy money to be made. In the future you will not have representatives who have an outside interest that clashes with their duty to their people. A different system of selection and qualification will have to be introduced. This will not be as difficult as it may sound, as in the future people will be known for their honesty and spirituality.

The model for all future political systems will be established in the United States and it will reflect the spiritual aspirations of the people. I talk here of Universal Laws that must be applied in the relationship between those ruling and the governed. People will have a far greater say in matters affecting them.

Once it can be seen that those appointed to act on your behalf are the right people, and can be trusted, life will quickly move on.

People all over the world are going to see the same changes within their ruling parties. If need be, whole governments will be removed, and control turned over to those who have the real interests of the people at heart.

One of the most noticeable changes will be in the area of decision making. Gone will be the political infighting that has often prevented desirable changes from being passed. A clear mandate will be given and matters of urgency will not be delayed. With new leaders it will soon be seen that they are true representatives of the people. Behind them will be a team of advisors that will be conversant with the plan that will carry Humanity forward.

Knowledge will be shared with all, and there will be no gain for any individual to personally profit from it. In fact, there will be a totally different outlook in such matters, and working for the good of all will be the main criterion. This is based upon spiritual concepts that will lift Humanity to a new level of awareness.

By then your media outlets will have been re-established and your news will be true and reliable, and there will be no need for censorship as there will be nothing to hide from you. What you see or hear in one part of the world will go to One Humanity worldwide.

9

Health

There is enough wealth in the world to provide FREE health-care. The care-givers however will change.

The monopoly of the pharmaceutical companies will be broken, and their products will have to be proven effective, and without side-effects, before they can be distributed to doctors, hospitals and the general public.

According to medical journals, less than 30% of pharmaceutical products receive any real testing at all before they are launched on an unsuspecting public.

Natural products will take their place, resulting soon in a reduction of the requirement for hospital beds, or allowing full use of current facilities. With the emphasis on preventive medicine, illness will drop drastically.

Medical Doctors will be obliged to take courses in Health (*merely an option in medical school - if one can believe that*). They must return to being the physicians of old, true Doctors of Health, rather than doctors of medicine.

Laboratories will produce natural remedies which have long been suppressed.

The role of Nurses in hospitals will be fully recognized and they will play a major role in returning patients to full health. Many of those displaced over the years will return to their profession.

Practitioners of alternative or complementary medicine will receive recognition for their expertise and ability to treat imbalances in the physical body. Prevention rather than cure will be the new byword in health care.

NESARA I

10
Science

Under constitutional law inventors of NEW ENERGY devices will be able to safely make their devices available publicly. Alternative medical therapies and technologies can also be made available without worry of attacks by FDA agents or other government interference. What a tremendous benefit to the human race!

One method that the Illuminati used to hamper the progress of science was to introduce systems and theories which prevented scientifically-useful measurements being made.

The introduction of the *metric system* was one such tool. It prevents advanced scientific calculations from being made accurately. Despite its seeming difficulty and lack of reason, the so-called "Imperial" system of weights and measures is much more accurate. We will therefore change back to using pounds rather than kilograms, although it will not be compulsory - some branches of industry might want to retain the metric system because of their business dealings with other countries which only use the metric system (at least for the moment).

Some changes were only nominal, so changing back to a 2 x 4 in the lumber industry would not be difficult.

In making this change it will be lawful to use volumetric measure only for liquids and gases. Apples and pears, for instance, will no longer be sold by the litre, as is done is some quarters today. This would seem to be a common sense rule.

NESARA I

11

Sports

Emphasis on amateur sports (for the sake of exercise rather than competition) will be greatly increased and significantly more funding made available for prospective Olympic and other athletes, as well as for school and university sports facilities. The funding will cover travel costs to international events.

The astronomical payments made today to players in competitive sports will be history. Back to the $1 entrance fee to the ballgame? And likewise in other countries the admission fee to popular sports will be reduced in similar fashion: investment (and gambling) will disappear from the sports field and professional players will be paid at a level more appropriate to the benefit they bring to the public. After the initial shock, the games will become more enjoyable to all.

In some sports (particularly ice-hockey) the audience has been attracted more by the on-field violence than the excellence of play itself, and the games have been orchestrated that way.

"Soccer hooligans" is a popular term in Europe especially as violence – not on the field, but amongst the spectators, has been a well-known aspect of the game for many years. It was noticeable however that the violence took place in games held fairly close to the sea. In Britain of course this meant all games and it was soon termed "The English Disease."

Nobody thought however of 'mind-control'. Russian

submarines patrolled The North Sea, the English Channel and the Eastern Atlantic, and beamed mind-controlling frequencies to areas where these games were held. I noticed this first when violence occurred in games held in Germany close to the coast – but not in Southern Germany, which was far from any open sea! It soon became obvious what was going on.

The European International Championship (Euro 2008) held in June of 2008 in Austria and Switzerland was not only far from the sea, but there was a distinct change in attitude amongst fans. There was not a single act of violence – quite extraordinary – and there were even incidents of quite opposite emotions. The Dutch team took out a full-page ad in the local Berne newspaper thanking the people of Berne and Switzerland for their hospitality.

Was this really soccer? Hopefully an indication of the many positive changes that are taking place worldwide as we start to welcome in this Golden Age.

12
Technology

Science will take on a new meaning as new technologies are released, radically changing the way we do things.

Oil and gas will no longer be used, or at least drastically reduced: plastics are still useful. Oil tankers will become redundant. Gas-lines will no longer be required.

Power lines will disappear - no more blemishes on the countryside.

Nuclear power will be dropped like a hot potato.

Even energies which seemed to be the answer will be dropped - hydrogen, bio-diesel, wind-power, solar power. Cosmic energies are so much simpler, available in the atmosphere around us - and free.

The use of cosmic energy will be one of the greatest contributions to environmental wellbeing on this planet. Only renewable, environmentally-friendly energies will be used.

NESARA I

13
Transportation

Production of non-fossil fuels for propulsion, the transportation industry will enjoy a new lease on life. There will be an initial collapse, of course, but it will be reborn with renewed vigour. Fuel costs, including related taxes, constitute a major portion of the operating costs of air, sea and land transportation companies. No more bankrupt airlines.

Rail will emerge once again as an economical means of transporting bulk and heavy goods, as well as reviving the romantic aspect of travel by rail.

Fresh investment would be made in rail stock, in railway stations, in railroads in general, and past abandoned lines would be reopened. It has long been treated by government as the Cinderella of the transportation industry, whereas in places like Europe, it is a favourite means of efficient, clean and comfortable transportation.

All special taxes on travel, especially airport and security taxes, which sometimes amount to 30% or more of the cost of travel, would be eliminated. It is not yet quite clear whether the new sales tax on non-essential goods and services would be applied to travel: the probability is that it would not. Travel on business would be considered essential; private travel - well, rest and relaxation is an essential part of healthy living, so this should also be exempt.

The eventual elimination of fossil fuels would contribute greatly to a pollution-free environment on land, in the sea and in the air. Preparations for elimination of all pollution in air transportation are already underway.

There are formulations for removing pollution from water using structured water and similar systems.

Electron charge-cluster technology and anti-gravity devices will form the basis for free-energy propulsion systems.

Much of this can be read in *The Journal of New Energy* edited by Hal Fox, whose company E.E.M.F. (Emerging Energies Marketing Firm) will have a useful head start in this field. His laboratory is recognized as the foremost on the planet in terms of new-energy device development.

It will be quite a challenge to meet the need for these new-energy devices, particularly conversion kits for conventional vehicles, tapping into space energies - how many automobiles, trucks and off-the-road vehicles are operating worldwide today? How many ships are operating on the high seas and inland waterways? How many jet aircraft and general aircraft are flying worldwide? Such a market is hard to comprehend. When one thinks of all the traditional industries which will cease to exist, it is easy to see that even more jobs will be created by new industries.

Marine operations would especially benefit from new, clean means of propulsion, but it would eliminate much of the need for oil and gas tankers, which would be refurbished for other purposes or scrapped.

One of the principal sources for energy would be the atmosphere itself.

Going back to the 'fifties, when Nikola Tesla drove a

vehicle around New York City without the use of gasoline. The demand will be so great that each country will be producing their own, helping to negate the loss of jobs in other industries. The military have been using acvanced technology for decades, against their fellow-citizens, but now the tables will be turned, and the technology will be put to good use — and the military put out to pasture.

In the meantime, what will happen to the petroleum industry? We imagine that there would be severe penalties initially for price-fixing over the past decades; that the price of a litre of gas would go back to 5c, a US gallon to 20c (the prices I remember in the gas wars of 1971); or the industry would be nationalised and low prices prevail until there was no further need for gas-stations. Aware of the dismal future outlook, prices at the gas pump are soaring at the moment to unheard of heights. Making hay while the sun shines.

There was great excitement about hydrogen some years back, and bio-diesel more recently, but these were interim measures and will fade. Automobile manufacturers are already producing hybrid vehicles - in deference to the petroleum industry (who have the same controllers), they have not yet made them *fully electric,* but there are engines waiting in the wings which will drink in only the atmosphere (*electron charge-coupled devices*) or hydrogen from the water in the very near future.

The Electrically Powered Flying Vehicle

Our highways are obsolete. Every year, millions of dollars are wasted on repairing a system that can no longer accommodate the transportation needs of the 21st century. And to make matters worse, our already overburdened highways are bombarded yearly with thousands and thousands of new drivers. Not only does this cause further highway destruction, but it worsens pollution and slows traffic. Maybe worst of all, it increases the likelihood of traffic fatalities. The Langenburg Research Center in Eugene Oregon has an alternative: the electrically powered flying vehicle."

In the meantime, tremendous steps forward have been taken in the introduction of new technologies (or hitherto secret ones). This will be the start of a new industrial revolution.

Apart from the cleanup of Mother Earth, specific interest was shown in building space-craft for transporting relief supplies and services to under-developed countries, to relieve famine and poverty. Once this has been done attention will be turned to transporting people and replacing commercial jet aircraft, especially jumbo-jets. This would collapse the airline industry and create an entirely new industry.

There have been some rational attempts made and achieved for the replacement of fossil fuels by the use of tidal power, wind power, and solar energy.

We applaud these changes, however, it is much more important to use some of the new technology that we shall have available to tap into the non-polluting use of the vast energy of space. Space everywhere, on the ground, in the air, under the water, or in space away from Earth.

It is going to be an entirely different world - without global or industrial cartels.

14

War and Weapons of War

The elimination of war worldwide will have far-reaching effects. The purpose of the military will change. The munitions factories (*all holdings of the Illuminati, who have always organised war throughout the planet*) will close down or be converted to manufacturing products for more useful purposes.

Factories which produced weapons of war or 'mass destruction' will either close down or take part in space program activities, as attention is paid more to intergalactic communications, travel and relationships.

NESARA I

15
The Weather

Right now weather across the world is out of control, or at least contrary to expectations.

Many of the severe weather systems in recent years were man-created weather wars (*forecast back in the '80s*). This has unbalanced the natural system worldwide.

Although intense storms, flooding, fires and other disasters had been forecast for the future, as well as major changes in climatic conditions, most of that scenario, however, has been changed. The fierce fires in California and other places were man-engineered to redirect our attention away from other important events that were occurring.

The December 2004 major tsunami in SW Asia was partly man-engineered, but it is claimed that that will be the last one that man has a hand in. There will be one or two others of a lesser nature as Mother Earth continues to adjust herself. There were also pre-arranged agreements for many to depart this life at this point in time.

Update June 2008: for some time now there have been warnings of extreme seismic activity and tsunamis, particularly on the West Coast of North America. **These have been held back for some time by the Celestials, or their severity lessened, but sooner or later they will become a reality.** Some of this activity may happen during 'stasis'. There are areas which are and can be protected, depending upon the Lightworkers in that area, but those who do not feel inclined to move from their current location may choose to remain there - unless and until they receive instructions from within to do otherwise.

Some important areas may indeed receive damage, but will receive funding to rebuild – and the opportunity to acquire property at a more advantageous price. '

16
Freedom of the Press

A detailed history and the extent to which there has been NO freedom of the press is given on this web page, for the benefit primarily of those who for some time have been oblivious to this.

Controlling all media was an important step in preventing the public from accessing real information and thereby maintaining controlling the public. The same is also true of the education system.

The introduction of the internet soon began to create problems for the Illuminati as there is no control over what is published on the internet – although there have been several attempts to do so, some partially successful. It was easier to spread the rumour that information found on the internet was false and misleading as it did not come from 'authoritative' sources. Many still hold that opinion – only when they see it on TV or in 'the press' will they believe it ….. that goes hand-in-hand with the belief that 'the government will take care of me' …… yes, but not in the way you think they will!

Upon the announcement all this will change. Many in the media cannot wait for this to happen, and many have been leading supporters of NESARA. Some, regrettably, have passed on in the meantime. Whether control over existing media outlets will fall to Lightworkers or whether new channels will be created is not yet known, but either way, the situation will change overnight. It is anticipated that there will be Celestial involvement here, especially in the announcement itself.

Comte de Saint Germain
"A man who knows everything and who never dies,"
- Voltaire

17

St. Germain & The Nesara Trusts

The story of how this change will occur, takes us back to Tudor England. There was an enigmatic character by the name of Saint Germain.

He learned the secrets of alchemy. By studying ancient esoteric knowledge into the occult, he was literally able to turn lead into gold, rocks into diamonds, and later was able transmute his mortal body into an immortal angel conquering death itself. With his "elixir of life" and positive thinking he never aged at all.

> "It is the activity of our nerves, the flame of our desire, the acid of our fears, which daily consume our organism. He who succeeds in raising himself above his emotions, in suppressing in himself anger and the fear of illness, is capable of overcoming the attrition of the years, and attaining an age at least double that at which men now die of old age." — *Saint Germain.*

Comte de Saint Germain was noted for rubbing elbows with the monarchies. Many of which commented on his elaborate shoes stubbed with $40,000 diamonds and pearls. No one knew the source of his income. Then around 1727 he shared his secret money making techniques with certain German bankers in hopes that they would use the money to help humanity.

Using his techniques, they along with the monarchies choose to squander the money for themselves. Even to this day, these bankers have continued to keep this knowledge secret.

Eventually Saint Germain realized the money was never going to be used for benevolent purposes so he pulled his money out, and in 1729 he put it into his own "World Trust." At the founding of the trust it was stipulated that this money would be released in the year 2000.

Bank Roll Programs

Around the turn of the century, the children of robber barons, and "banksters" began to see the error in their parent's evilness and their use of wealth. These 100 children are known as "wealthy visionaries". Together they invested some of their families money into secret money roll programs, to be used for humanitarian purposes.

The bank roll programs, allow wealthy investors to make insane profits by ripping off the assets and resources from third world nations. The profits from these programs are utterly astronomical as monthly returns can be in excess of 1:100,000 and 1:500,000. The name "roll programs" comes from a method of rolling money over and over in short periods of time. At the end of each cycle investors then reinvest or "roll" the principle and interest earned over into the next cycle. In the late 1990's the bank roll programs finally ceased.

Money earned from these bank roll programs became known as the "Prosperity Programs" Over time the programs where secretly opened up to small investors so that one could invest as little as one hundred dollars at a time. These small amounts where handled by trustees, who collected the money and kept records, and combined the small investments into the large amount, let's say, one million dollars, that was required in order to enter a "roll".

The news of these programs spread by word of mouth and especially via multi-level marketers. Thousands of people invested and great wealth was generated, but little, if anything was ever paid back to the investors. Trustees such as Clyde Hood and Mike Kadoski where sent to jail under false charges. Then corruption, greed, and fraud became wide spread among the bankers, government, and even some trustees who wanted to steal the money for themselves. Even the Bush family had their hands in the pot, using Promis Software they could transfer stolen funds without being traced. Many have died because of this wealth, but God has another plan for humanity.

The Time Has Now Come

The time has now come to release these Prosperity Funds and the funds from Saint Germain's, World Trust. This money will be used to buy out all oil corporations, banks, pharmaceutical cartels, and zero out all debt. 250 years of compound interest has mushroomed the World Trust into a net worth in excess of one quattuordecillion dollars, that's 1 with 40 zeros behind it, or $1,000,000,000,000,000,000,000,000,000,000,000,000,000,000.

This is enough money to buy a gold cube the size of the orbit of Saturn. So astronomical most people will not believe it!

The money from the World Trust will be distributed in the following manner.

Level One — The World Trust under the trustee-ship of Master St. Germain. At his direction The World Trust can only be activated for payout only two times during any given year, Easter and Christmas. At St. Germain's orders the World Court activates the funding process. This process continues down through the four lower levels of trusts to the people, and under certain conditions the funding window remains open until the next holiday funding window begins. For example, if the Easter window is activated, the window can remain open until December 24, the day before Christmas, at which time it closes. The window remains open only if signifi-cant funds are moved to certain designated trusts dur-ing a set period of time. If not, the funding window is closed when such deadlines are not met.

Level Two — 180 Royal Trusts under the control of trustees in various sovereign countries. Examples are The French Trust, The Russian Trust, and the Vatican Trust.

Level Three — The Family Trusts under the con-trol of trustees of the world's wealthiest families. Examples are Bronfman, Warburg, Morgan, Rothschild, and Rockefeller.

Level Four -- 250 plus Corporate Trusts under the control of trustees from powerful companies and corporations. Examples are General Electric, Lockheed, General Motors, Boeing, Carnegie, Ford, Marriott and AT&T. There are 4-5 trustees per trust which means that approximately 1200 trustees must sign documents to move money through these trusts.

Level Five — The Prosperity Program Trusts which represent the various 70-75 bank roll programs which are under the control of designated program trustees. Again, there are 4-5 trustees per trust or some 350 persons who must sign documents to activate these trusts. Some examples include Bergevene, SBC, ITI, Savage, Morgan, Omega, and Freedom. The largest trust is Freedom and it must be funded first. It is these trust's that hold the wealth from the enlighten robber baron children.

Finally Release

Finally the funds will be released to the common man. As the funds pass through each trust, the trustee must use only certain designated "safe" banks and sign the proper documents with only certain designated banking personnel at those banks. Should this process be activated, and then be stalled by deceitful bankers, deceitful trustees, etc. and the deadlines for funding to reach certain trusts are not met, the funding window is then closed. This is the problem; members of the Bush family are blocking the release of these funds

NESARA I

18

Spiritual Aspects of NESARA

We occasionally hear comments that NESARA is "not spiritual" because some people perceive that NE-SARA is only about money.

We are amused when we hear these comments because we know many people who consider themselves "spiritually-oriented", who constantly feel anxiety and fear because they don't have enough money to pay their bills.

These people are not able to pursue their spiritual desires to help improve the world because they are barely able to house, clothe and feed themselves; they work in jobs they do not find fulfilling, or they do work that barely brings them enough money to survive.

People often fail to appreciate that having enough money gives One more personal autonomy and energy to live One's spiritual values and take action to help humanity or the world. Many people have gotten confused by the wrong idea that "money is evil"; when in fact, "the LOVE of money is the root of all evil".

Or perhaps they think that being spiritual means to take a vow of poverty, consciously or unconsciously.

Money is "energy" and it is neutral; it can be used for good or for bad; but money, itself, is neutral. Money is the way we exchange our energy and time for something we need that has been created through the time and energy of other people.

When we look around to see what humanitarian activities are undertaken by those we consider to be spiritual, we inevitably see that these spiritual people use money to accomplish many of their humanitarian improvement projects.

The Christian organization known as Feed the Children raised $553 Million in cash and gifts, in 2002, and spent $514 Million to provide food, shelter, medical services, disaster relief, education, and other services to needy children and their communities around the world.

Whether it is a starving child in Africa, or a married couple in the United States, who are bickering about not having the money to pay their bills, and struggling to obtain food, shelter, and safety for their family, most people cannot be their "best" selves, in expressing their spiritual feelings. Lack of money keeps people from being as spiritual as they would like to be, due to anxiety, fear, frustration, and all the other emotions they experience in struggling to survive.

A famous expert, Maslow, helps us to understand that unless people have their basic needs met, they do not have the ability to focus on higher matters. Maslow's hierarchy of needs, listed below, helps us see that the basic needs, of hunger, thirst, safety, etc., must be satisfied before people can raise themselves to a higher status where they can live in harmony with others and also obtain self-esteem through their achievements.

Maslow's Hierarchy of Needs
http://tinyurl.com/4xaakrs

1) Physiological: hunger, thirst, bodily comforts, etc;

2) Safety/security: out of danger;

3) Belongingness and Love: affiliate with others, be accepted;and

4) Esteem: to achieve, be competent, gain approval and recognition.

NESARA immediately puts extra cash into Americans' pockets, by providing bank debt forgiveness and the abolishment of federal income taxes. The month of NESARA's announcement, Americans will stop paying income taxes and credit card debts, mortgages, car loans, education loans, and all other bank related debts as these are forgiven. The month of NESARA is announced will result in providing a windfall of cash in American's pockets in numerous ways.

NESARA also removes the current institutionalized robbery of people's money performed by the current banking systems. Due to high interest rates and compound interest which is unconstitutional, the Federal Reserve banking system is essentially stealing money from Americans every day.

NESARA provides many benefits which result in people having more money in their pockets. It will be easier for people to pay for their basic needs of food, shelter, and safety after NESARA is announced because most people will actually have more of the money they receive available to them to spend instead of paying income taxes and paying off bank debts. This increase in money will enable people to begin to lift themselves out of financial struggle and to have less anxiety and frustration due to lack of money. This can give them the peace of mind and energy to focus on their spiritual lives.

There is another benefit to NESARA that is not widely understood but which very definitely supports spiritual values. Are you aware that in the last few years since the 9/11 attacks, the Bush regime has instructed the FBI to label many good Americans as potential terrorists? In late 2001 and all through 2002, police departments around the country were being trained by NSA and FBI experts in how to spot potential terrorists. I recall one FBI regional office was putting out posters describing potential terrorists. Among those listed were any people who quote the Constitution and Christians who homeschool their children. The powers to interfere with Americans' lives are given in the Bush regime patriot act and follow-up legislation which are attacks on Americans' freedom.

NESARA will totally obliterate the misnamed patriot act and follow-up legislation as well as all legislation which has been attacking our Constitution and our civil rights. NESARA will restore to Americans their rights to pursue living their spiritual values and Americans will be encouraged to know the Constitution.

In addition, after NESARA's announcement, there will be vast amounts of humanitarian prosperity programs funds which will finally be released to be used for world improvements.

Because most of the world's banking systems are owned by the Illuminati, these funds have been kept from being released until after the banking law changes initiated by NESARA in the United States, and related international banking law changes can and will protect these vast funds. Literally millions of ordinary people will be receiving these funds and will be lawfully required to use these funds to improve the world.

The world improvement projects being funded by the prosperity programs will benefit people in need and our world in many ways. In addition, there will be need for people to staff the many improvement projects activities.

Spiritually-oriented people who wish to be involved in improvement projects will have opportunities to make money and fulfill their love of people, Spirit, and the planet by participating in these world improvement projects.

In addition, after NESARA is announced, there will be very spiritually uplifting news which will finally be televised and reported for the first time in modern history.

The truth about the true divinity of Earth Humans will become known in miraculous ways. This is all we can say about this subject at this time, however, there is MUCH MORE we will be able to discuss after NESARA's announcement. This grand news will ONLY BE POSSIBLE AFTER NESARA is announced.

We hope, perhaps, that now it's obvious *WHY* many of us see NESARA as primarily spiritual in nature, with down-to-Earth benefits which set a new foundation for a much better world.

NESARA Yes!

Blessings and Love.

19

Startling Facts Concerning 911

WTC 7 held all the records of fraud (all sorts) that involved people at Enron, and BUSH was part of the Enron fraud. It also had the antitrust suit against Microsoft. Coincidence? We don't think so . . .

Also, the towers required some $200 million in renovations and improvements, most of which related to removal and replacement of building materials declared to be health hazards in the years since the towers were built.

It was well-known by the city of New York that **the WTC was an asbestos bombshell**. For years, the Port Authority treated the building like an aging dinosaur, attempting on several occasions to get permits to demolish the building for liability reasons, but being turned down due to the known asbestos problem. Further, it was well-known the only reason the building was still standing until 911 was because it was too costly to disassemble the Twin Towers floor by floor since the Port Authority was prohibited legally from demolishing the buildings. "Dem-o-ing" it down would be much, much cheaper.

Larry Silverstein was the lease holder on the twin towers and bought it at $3.2 billion dollars and will soon collect $7.1 billion dollars or more. It's all about the money... he got his wish for a demolition and cost him nothing. "Weighing in at $3.2 billion, the acquisition of the 99-year leasehold of the World Trade Center was the largest of the year".

One other thing that the public did NOT know, the UN-Constitutional PATRIOT ACT was already written and was sitting on the shelf weeks before 9/11 happened.

The smoking gun are the BTS reports found on the www.bts.gov website that tracks every single flight going in and out, and flights 11 and 77 DID NOT fly that day whatsoever.

American Airline even confirmed this with an edit to http://tinyurl.com/6xfb5qv Wikipedia is NOT a place for 100% credible info, however, Wikipedia tracks all IP addresses that make corrections on the site. We even ran the IP address ourselves and indeed, American Airline did the edit for flights 11 and 77 on that day.

Is someone at AA trying to tell Americans something?

Lets look at some of the physical evidence.

Look at the image of the core's steal beams of the Twin Towers, on the left. It CLEARLY shows that Shape Charges were used to cut those beams **at a perfect angle,** so the towers could fall down on it's own footprints; and how the towers exploded outwards.

Then they go on to say that the building did a pancake effect, take a look at the picture on the next page, does that look to you like a pancake effect?

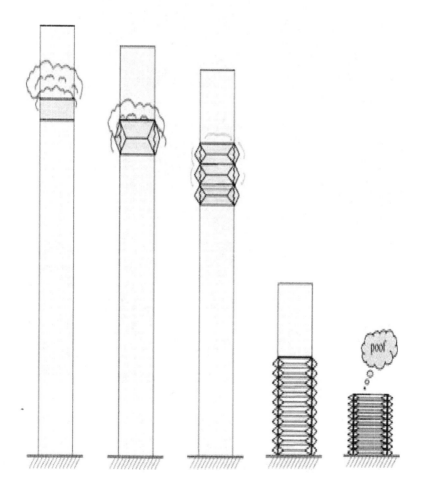

The biggest LIE is that a huge jumbo jet hit the pentagon with NO damage to the lawn while flying **super low** to the ground (without the massive turbine engines scraping the lawn) where the nose of the plane hit, IM-POSSIBLE! Just look at the picture and I rest my case.

Rumsfeld admitted to $2.3 trillion missing on September 10, 2001 (the day before 9/11) and where the "plane" hit, took out the servers.

911 was clearly staged, especially with them having insiders standing ready with video camera's to catch the first plane to hit. However, we all know by now that the video feeds given to the news were altered and faked.

Since 911, our Constitutional rights have been systematically dismantled: (partial list)

1. **USA Patriot Act** - A 342 page document presented to Congress one day before voting on it that allows the government access to your bank and email accounts, as well as your medical and phone records with no court order. They can also search your home anytime without a warrant.

2. **USA Patriot Act II** - This one allows secret government arrests, the legal authority to seize your American citizenship, and the extraction of your DNA if you are deemed a potential terrorist.

3. **Military Commissions Act of 2006** - Ends habeas corpus, the right to an attorney, and the right to court review of one's detention and arrest. Without this most basic right, all other rights are gone too since anyone can be detained indefinitely. Now anyone may be arrested and incarcerated and nobody would know.

4. **NSPD 51** - A directive signed by George W. Bush on May 9, 2007, that allows the President to declare martial law, effectively transforming the U.S. into a dictatorship with no checks and balances from the Legislative or Judicial Branches. Parts of this directive are considered classified and members of Congress have been denied the right to review it.

5. **Protect America Act of 2007** - Allows unprecedented domestic wiretapping and surveillance activities with a reduction in FISA court oversight. Probable cause is not needed.

6. **John Warner Defense Authorization Act** - Signed by George W. Bush on October 17, 2007, this act allows the President to declare a public emergency and station troops anywhere in America without the consent of the governor or local authorities to "suppress public disorder.

7. **Homegrown Terrorism and Radicalization Act** - Passed overwhelmingly by Congress on October 23, 2007, is now awaiting a Senate vote. This act will beget a new crackdown on dissent and the Constitutional rights of American citizens. The definitions of "terrorism" and

"extremism" are so vague that they could be used to generalize against any group that is working against the policies of the Administration. In this bill, "violent radicalization" criminalizes thought and ideology while "homegrown terrorism" is defined as "the planed use of force to coerce the government." The term, "force" could encompass political activities such as protests, marches, or any other form of non-violent resistance.

So when you add in:

1. **Halliburton Confirms Camps Constructed** (Over 3,700 FEMA camps in America, FOR WHAT?!?!)
2. **Halliburton's Immigrant Detention Centers**
3. **Homeland Security Contracts for Vast New Detention Camps**
4. **Halliburton Confirms Concentration Camps Already Constructed**
5. **KBR awarded Homeland Security contract worth up to $385M**
6. **This from Halliburton's own website**

The latest from is Cybersecurity Act (S. 773) **http://www.govtrack.us/congress/bill.xpd?bill=s111-773** A new Cyber security bill would grant the President unprecedented power to shut down the internet and ignore privacy laws. This bill was written by no other than one of the infamous rockefeller family member. **http://www.youtube.com/watch?v=Ct9xzXUQLuY** Watch "Internet should have never been invented"

Where did the term "Al-Qaeda" come from?

Former British Foreign Secretary Robin Cook wrote that the word **Al-Qaeda** should be translated as **"the**

database", and originally referred to the computer file of the thousands of mujahideen militants who were recruited and trained with CIA help to defeat the Russians.

Power is an elusive thing. It is ultimately a fine balance of mass psychology built up through the momentum of the past. Changing the very top of the world's power structure involves a shift in the psychology of the people who rule the planet. That change is then followed by a change in public announcements and actions. People watching the collapse of the current world regime are getting impatient because it seems to be taking so much time. They need to understand that changing a system that has existed for thousands of years needs to be handled with great care in order to avoid chaos, starvation and war. Nonetheless, the signs of global regime change are everywhere.

NESARA I

"To those leaning on the sustaining Infinite, to-day is big with blessings. The wakeful shepherd beholds the first faint morning beams, ere cometh the full radiance of a risen day. So shone the pale star to the prophet shepherds; yet it traversed the night, and came where, in cradled obscurity, lay the Bethlehem babe, the human herald of Christ, Truth, who would make plain to benighted understanding the way of salvation through Christ Jesus, till across a night of error should dawn the morning beams and shine the guiding star of being. The Wisemen were led to behold and to follow this daystar of divine Science, lighting the way to eternal harmony.

"The time for thinkers has come."

— Science and Health with Key to the Scriptures,
by Mary Baker Eddy (1821-1910)

NESARA I

Everyone Is Welcome

Everyone is welcome to enjoy the refuge of the The United States of America — regardless of race, color, nationality, or creed, in the spirit of Jesus Christ — for it is written . . .

"Come unto me, all ye that labor and are heavy laden, and I will give you rest."

Matthew 11:28.

NESARA I

Christian Obligations

"Unto everyone that hath shall be given, and he shall have abundance: but from him that hath not shall be taken away even that which he hath." — *Christ Jesus, at Matthew 25:29.*

It is necessary and proper, now, to lay the plans and strategy for establishing an American standard of living higher than we have ever known before.

As a Christian nation, we cannot be content, no matter how high that general standard of living may be, if some fraction of our people — whether it be one-third or one-fifth or one-tenth — is ill-fed, ill-clothed, ill-housed, and insecure.

This Republic had its beginning, and grew to its present strength, under the protection of certain, inalienable, political rights — among them the right of *free speech, free press, free worship, freedom from unreasonable searches and seizures, and trial by jury*.

These were and are our rights to liberty and life.

As our nation has grown in size and stature, however, — as our industrial economy expanded — these *political rights* must be enhanced by the *voluntary obligations* of Christian Brotherhood.

We have come to a clear realization of the fact that true individual freedom cannot exist without economic independence and security. *"Necessitous men are not free men."*(*Vernon v Bethell,* 28 ER 838,1762). People who are hungry and lacking meaningful occupation are the stuff of which dictatorships are made.

In our day these economic truths have become accepted as self-evident. We have accepted, today, the *voluntary obligations* of which we speak, under which a new basis of security and prosperity can be established for all — regardless of station, race, or creed.

Among these necessities are:

1. The necessity for a useful and remunerative occupation in the industries or shops or farms or mines or homes of the nation;

2. The necessity to acquire enough to provide adequate food and clothing and recreation;

3. The necessity of every farmer to raise and sell his products at a return which will give him and his family a decent living;

4. The necessity of every businessman, large and small, to trade in an atmosphere of freedom from unfair competition and domination by monopolies at home or abroad;

5. The necessity of every family to a decent home;

6. The necessity for adequate medical care and the opportunity to achieve and enjoy good health;

7. The necessity for adequate protection from the economic fears of sickness, accident, unemployment, and old age;

8. The necessity for a good education.

All of these necessities spell security.

So we must be prepared to move forward — in the implementation of these necessities — to new goals of human endeavor, well-being and happiness.

This Republic's rightful place in the world depends in large part upon how fully these and similar necessities are fulfilled, in practice, for all our citizens. For unless there is security here at home, there cannot be lasting peace in the world.

Too many times the "church" has refused to take righteous political action, hiding behind their cowardice of 501(c)3 tax exemption.

We must abandon the fatal ideology of Separation of Church and State. It was the intent of the Founding Fathers to keep the Church from influencing the State. It was their intent to keep the State from influencing the Church. However, the State now controls the Church, but the Church no longer influences the State.

We cannot pass laws forcing people to live righteously, but we can pass laws to keep them from inflicting their evil upon society. That is the goal of The Maine free State and why we heartedly endorse and encourage your participation in The Republic for the united States of America.

NESARA I

"My God shall supply all your need according to his riches in glory by Christ Jesus."
— *Phillipians 4:19.*

NESARA I

According to the Federal Reserve Act of 1913, "All present and succeeding debt against the US Treasury must be assumed by the Federal Reserve." (p.13)

NESARA I

After the Civil War, the Government allowed citizens to claim a payment on anyone who suffered damages as a result of the Federal Government for failing to protect its citizens from harm of damages by a foreign government. (p.14)

A claim of harm can be made on any loan issued by any financial institution, for all interest paid, foreclosures, attorney and court fees, IRS taxes or liens, Real Estate and property taxes, mental and emotional stress caused by the loss of property, stress related illnesses such as suicide and divorce, and even warrants, incarceration, and probation, could also be claimed. (p.18)

NESARA I

For Extended Coverage
See NESARA II

Other Publications

NESARA: National *Economic Security
and Reformation Act*
http://tinyurl.com/c8u42q6

History of Banking: *An Asian Perspective*
http://tinyurl.com/boeehjl

The People's Voice: *Former Arizona
Sheriff Richard Mack*
http://tinyurl.com/d62fyg3

Asset Protection: *Pure Trust Organizations*
http://tinyurl.com/btrjfqp

The Matrix As It Is: *A Different Point Of View*
http://tinyurl.com/ckrbkge

From Debt To Prosperity: *'Social Credit' Defined*
http://tinyurl.com/d2tjmw3

Give Yourself Credit: *Money Doesn't Grow On Trees*
http://tinyurl.com/d7tphuv

My Home Is My Castle: *Beware Of The Dog*
http://tinyurl.com/bmzxc2n

Commercial Redemption: *The Hidden Truth*
http://tinyurl.com/d9etg7w

Hardcore Redemption-In-Law: *Commercial Freedom And
Release*
http://tinyurl.com/cl65vrz

Oil Beneath Our Feet: *America's Energy Non-Crisis*
http://tinyurl.com/btlzqxf

Untold History Of America: *Let The Truth Be Told*
http://tinyurl.com/bu9kjjc

Debtocracy: *& Odious Debt Explained*
http://tinyurl.com/cooqzuz

New Beginning Study Course: *Connect The Dots And See*
http://tinyurl.com/cxpk42p

Monitions of a Mountain Man: *Manna, Money, & Me*
http://tinyurl.com/cusgcqs

Maine Street Miracle: *Saving Yourself And America*
http://tinyurl.com/d4yktlw

Reclaim Your Sovereignty: *Take Back Your Christian Name*
http://tinyurl.com/cf5taxh

Gun Carry In The USA: Your Right To Self-defence
http://tinyurl.com/cdn3y3y

Climategate Debunked: *Big Brother, Main Stream Media*
http://tinyurl.com/d6gy2xz

Epistle to the Americans I: *What you don't
know about The Income Tax*
http://tinyurl.com/d99ujzm

Epistle to the Americans II: *What you don't
know about American History*
http://tinyurl.com/cnyghyz

Epistle to the Americans III: *What you don't
know about Money*
http://tinyurl.com/cp8nrh8

Made in the USA
Middletown, DE
18 June 2020